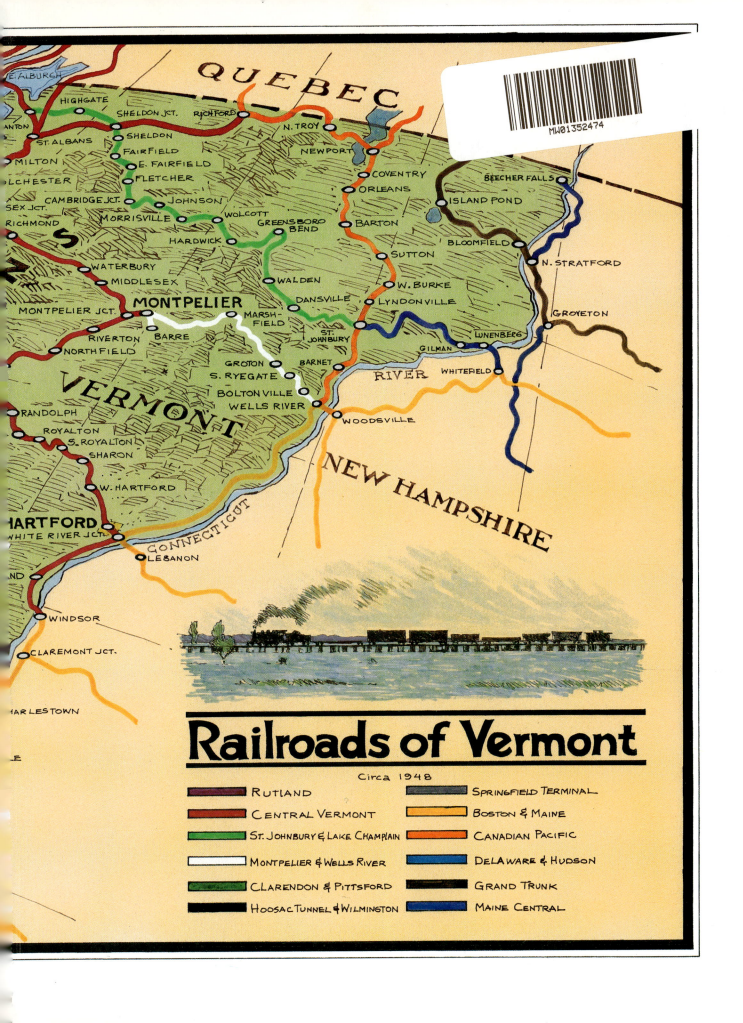

GREEN MOUNTAIN RAILS

Vermont's Colorful Trains

Vermont's Colorful Trains

by Robert Willoughby Jones

Pine Tree Press - Los Angeles, California

FRONT COVER: Central Vermont's 2-8-0 No. 460 highballing out of Brattleboro on a brilliant winter day epitomizes all that is both rugged and beautiful about Vermont's railroads. Photographed on January 9, 1951 by Stephen R. Payne.

REAR COVER ABOVE: Three of the GE 70-tonners owned by the St. Johnsbury & Lamoille County round the bend as they work their way down into St. Johnsbury in May 1966. J. Emmons Lancaster collection.

REAR COVER BELOW: This is what up-country railroading looked like for a hundred years. Rutland 4-6-0 No. 74 is working at North Bennington on August 14, 1952. Stephen R. Payne photo.

FRONTISPIECE: Never was steam more comfortable in a winter landscape. Grand Trunk 2-8-2 No. 3432 is assisting Central Vermont 2-8-0 No. 470 in climbing Roxbury Hill near Montpelier Junction in December 1956 with a long freight. The Mike cut off at the top of the hill while the 470 continued on with the train. "A wicked cold day, as the term goes hereabouts," according to photographer David C. Bartlett.

OPPOSITE TABLE OF CONTENTS: From July 5, 1952 we have this nicely framed portrait of a milk train southbound at Colchester. John Gardner photo.

FRONT END PAPER: The Railroads of Vermont as they existed circa 1948. John Signor is the artist.

REAR END PAPER: The *Montrealer* departs Essex Junction into the black of the night for Montreal. Jim Shaughnessy photo.

GREEN MOUNTAIN RAILS—Vermont's Colorful Trains

© 1994 by Robert Willoughby Jones. All rights reserved.

No part of this book may be used or reproduced without written permission
from the publisher, except in the case of brief quotations used in reviews.

Layout and design by the author, based on original concepts by Katie Danneman
Cover design by Katie Danneman and Paul Hammond
Chapter head illustrations by Pamela Jones Aamodt
Color separations by Quad Color, Burbank, California
Printing and Binding by Walsworth Publishing Company, Marceline, Missouri
Manufactured in the United States of America
First Printing: Spring 1994

ISBN 0-9640356-0-X
Published by Pine Tree Press
P. O. Box 39484, Los Angeles, California 90039

In memory of Norton D. Clark

whose collection of photography and artifacts has captured an era for posterity

TABLE OF CONTENTS

     Foreword 8

     Acknowledgements 9

     Introduction 10

I   **Rutland** 13

        Vermont Railway
        Green Mountain Railroad

II   **Central Vermont** 59

III **St. Johnsbury & Lake Champlain** 117

        St. Johnsbury & Lamoille County
        Lamoille Valley Railroad

IV **In Granite Country** 125

        Montpelier & Wells River
        Barre & Chelsea
        Montpelier & Barre

V   **Country Cousins** 131

        Clarendon & Pittsford
        Hoosac Tunnel & Wilmington
        Springfield Terminal

VI **City Cousins** 143

        Boston & Maine
        Canadian Pacific
        Delaware & Hudson
        Grand Trunk
        Maine Central
        Amtrak

     Bibliography 174

     Index 175

FOREWORD

By Jim Shaughnessy

The land is aflame with autumn on October 12, 1991, as Vermont Railway GP38-2 No. 202 leads a freight across the Waloomsac River between North Bennington and Hoosick Junction. Jim Shaughnessy photo.

Why Vermont? Mountain climbers claim "just because it's there," but Vermont somehow goes beyond that simple explanation.

There seems to exist in this land a complicated combination of geography, history, emotion, and people. When you cross the state line and see the sign "Welcome to Vermont," there is an immediate sense of gratification that says this is the way the world should be.

When I was a youngster, my family were riders. We would often ride in the car somewhere on Sunday after church and frequently it would be to Vermont. A favorite route would be from Troy, our home, to Bennington, then up to Rutland, over to Whitehall at the south end of Lake Champlain and then back home. This, of course, gave me the opportunity to become familiar with the trains of the Rutland and Delaware & Hudson. The New York-bound *Green Mountain Flyer* and *Laurentian* would usually be encountered on their respective lines at some point. Weekend and summer jaunts broadened my horizons to Central Vermont, St. Johnsbury & Lake Champlain, and Boston & Maine—White River Junction was a particularly thrilling destination. Here the afternoon activities were wonderful, and not far out of town in any direction were the tranquil rural settings along the Connecticut and White Rivers that are the heart of the Vermont mystique.

These are the events that introduced me to and formed my impressions of Vermont.

All Vermont's rail lines are single track (except a seven-mile stretch of the B&M in Pownal) and it was on these winding paths that mixed trains of the Montpelier & Wells River and the St. Johnsbury & Lake Champlain were in their proper element. Even a diesel-powered mixed train was a thing of beauty. The smallest of depots in the obscure hills was the gateway to the world for those willing to venture forth.

All Vermont's trains were personable whether they were passenger or freight. Each town had its reason for the train to pause, whether it was a little depot, a creamery, or a grain mill. Most people's lives were touched even if it were only to pause at the barn door and watch the cars roll through the valley.

Ironically all the major historic rail routes in Vermont are still in place but their use has been sorrowfully curtailed. It is, however, still a thrill to see the cars rolling through the Winooski Valley or over the spine of the Green Mountains near Mt. Holly.

Now we have a chance, through these pages, to step back to the glory days and relive a special moment that many of us savored in a place it could only happen—*that's* why Vermont!

ACKNOWLEDGEMENTS

Creating this book has been a special pleasure for me. Not only have I had the opportunity for yet more trips to New England, and meeting new friends and renewing old acquaintances, I have also had the rare gift of an intensive look, through color photography, of a fascinating rail network in that unique place, Vermont. I have loved every foot and every moment of exploration in the Green Mountain State, though I cannot say these travels have been exhaustive or even extensive. But my experiences there took hold of me from the very start in a way I cannot adequately describe. Vermont works its own special magic. It has cast its spell on many of you, I know.

The 30 photographers represnted here have demonstrated their appreciation for the excitement of interesting railroading in a naturally spectacular setting, often in weather conditions demanding long patience and stamina, particularly during the cold months.

I was generously loaned hundreds of transparencies for this book. Some may wonder why I chose one particular image over another. Sheer caprice. I look for the unusual, and as a hopeless romantic I'm a sucker for lush scenery.

Togther let us salute those behind the lens:

Jack Armstrong	Arthur E. Mitchell
David C. Bartlett	Russell F. Munroe
Norton D. Clark	Leon Onofri
Mike Confalone	Charles G. Parsons
Stanley W. Cook	Stephen R. Payne
H. Bentley Crouch	Donald S. Robinson
T. J. Donahue	John Ross
David Engman	Richard B. Sanborn
John Gardner	Jim Shaughnessy
Albert G. Hale	Beatrice Smith
Al Irwin	Dwight A. Smith
Preston S. Johnson	Stanley Smith
Ronald N. Johnson	Alan W. Styffe
John F. Kane	David Sweetland
J. Emmons Lancaster	Alan Thomas
Fred H. Matthews	George W. Turnbull
George D. Melvin	Sandy Worthen

Too, I wish that photos could embrace more of the human saga in railroading, because certainly it's about more than just pretty pictures. The dedication of railroaders is sometimes overlooked. Their individual pains and passions surely do absorb us, yet we may gloss over this when looking at pictures. Railroading can be brutally tough work. Try to imagine the myriad stories behind each photo in this book. My fervent hope is that these images move you as much as they do me.

Several colleagues took time to review portions of the manuscript, for which I am indeed grateful: Edward A. Lewis, Donald S. Robinson, Mac Sebree, Jim Shaughnessy, Dwight A. Smith, Gary Webster, and Rick Welles.

My timetable collection has swelled appreciably due to the good offices of Arnold Joseph and Carl Loucks, both dealers in railroad paper. Several colorful items were loaned by the Conway Scenic Railway. The many tickets illustrated throughout are from Jack May's impressive collection, which he graciously offered without limit. Howard Moulton was of special help in finding the RPO indicia. George Carpenter and William Nixon opened their large collections of slides.

I am very grateful to Pentrex and its President, Mike Clayton, for their leading role in the book's distribution. Both Katie Danneman and Paul Hammond have been terrific in leading me through the production mine fields.

My beautiful sister, Pamela Jones Aamodt, has again brought her extraordinary talents to the creation of the chapter head illustrations, which she did so memorably in my earlier book on the Boston & Maine.

The past several years have been economically trying for Americans everywhere. The climate has not been encouraging for the publication of nostalgic color rail books. It is therefore all the more important that I acknowledge the courageous backers of this book who have advanced the many thousands of dollars necessary for its creation. I appreciate their confidence more than I can say. That you bought this book is your vote of confidence as well, and I thank my readers for their support.

Who can deny the visceral power of a train? T. J. Donahue caught a Central Vermont way freight headed south behind 2-8-0 No. 470.

INTRODUCTION

Railroads took hold of America in a dramatic way in circumstances difficult for us to contemplate today. The fear of every city, town, and village was that prosperity would pass by if it failed to have rails connecting with the outside world. No one envisioned the conveyance yet to be produced by the advent of the internal combustion engine, simply because there were no adequate roads. Roads were made of dirt, they suffered badly in inclement weather, and they were interminably slow. Because there was no vehicle needing an improved road system, no one conceived there could be one.

Moreover, in Vermont, virtually every foot of rail laid held the hope that *this* route would carry the profitable bridge traffic between the Great Lakes and the Atlantic Ocean. This commerce would surely help stem the tide of emigration out of Vermont which had become so serious in the early 1800s. Successful Vermont businessmen envisioned their state as the conduit of lakes-to-sea rail commerce. Contemporary newspapers produced copious quantities of pro-railroad prose, so assertive that there was really no question that such a rail line would be put down, it was just a matter of where, and therein lies a tale.

Vermonters are a hardy race of people. It could only be thus with these severe extremes of climate causing so tough a life. The meek either never went there, or they moved on after embracing its nature. To the outsider, Vermont is a paradise of scenery so intensely beautiful as almost to escape description, every season brilliant with individual splendor. To the native, it can be a place of unforgiving hardness. Today's Vermonter of longstanding heritage resents the rich newcomer who settles here for the beauty and quiet. The native would rather have more industry to create jobs and the better standard of living these bring. We outsiders pray that this still pristine state won't be further compromised. But what a paradox this is! We who love railroads, imagine how damaging they were to the wilderness. Indeed, the coming of the railroads in Vermont set in motion the virtual eradication of mountain forests by an over-stimulated logging industry.

Vermont's physical attributes have always bred independence of thought and spirit. W. Storrs Lee said that those who came here "wanted only the freedom of a virgin land." Ethan Allen is the name we remember with the Green Mountain Boys, stalwart defenders of early American independence who bluffed the British into surrendering Fort Ticonderoga. Yet Allen was merely the most outspoken of capable leaders then. It was the Boys themselves, men of every profession and calling, from whom the durable Vermont stock has descended. They bred generations of adventurers; after 1850—and even more after the Civil War—vast numbers left the state to pursue unknown challenges in the west. By 1900 some two-fifths of the population had migrated to other states.

Vermont lived by its villages and their general stores, centers of commerce, where the shopkeeper was the respected leader and arbiter. The political idea defining Vermont is that of distributing power widely. Its end is the town meeting, sacred form of government here, often arduous in execution, yet always the fairest which people could manage. It broke only for lunch and for the four o'clock milking time. To their everlasting credit, Vermonters outlawed slavery from their first constitution. The Republican Party at its 1854 formation denounced slavery heartily, and Vermont stepped aboard. Indeed, Lawrence Brainerd, major backer of the Vermont & Canada Railroad, was the first state senator sent to Washington to oppose slavery. It seemed ordained by God that Vermont should remain Republican.

Vermonters got their spirit of independence from their English roots. They strove to be self-sufficient, to create in the home what was needed. Home industries expanded into village industries, and most goods could be produced locally.

But home industry soon moved to the factory. At the same time the business of serious forest clearing had begun. Clear land was a settler's imperative if crops were to be grown and livestock raised. Vast tracts of field and hillside went up in flames as locals worked toward this now lamentable ideal. Some entrepreneurial fellow discovered that the ashes yielded potash, a product that soon became in heavy demand for Great Britain's glass and textile manufacturing. When this trade evaporated after nearly a century as Europeans discovered a cheaper substitute, Vermonters switched to the whiskey trade and its quick profits—some 200 distilleries worth. It wasn't until the 1830s that the temperance movement eventually quelled the ardor of the distillers—and the consumers.

All the while one Ira Allen had begun what was to become a sawmill empire. Its first conduit to market was a water route starting on the Winooski River into Lake Champlain and eventually to Quebec. Later the Connecticut River helped build an even more lucrative market in Massachusetts and Connecticut, and the coming of the railroads fanned these fires even more mightily. Burlington eventually became the No. 3 lumbering center in the country.

When the citizenry came to realize in the first decade of the 1900s just how badly Vermont had been damaged by the over-lumbering, it was too late; the forests were gone forever. Ever resourceful, they retooled the lumber operations to make practical use of their wood for furniture and a host of useful wood products. It was after the Depression cut deeply into even these businesses that the Vermonter once again discovered the value—and need—of home industry. This was the rebirth of the hand-crafted item and its importance to Vermont's economy today.

Through these changes Vermonters adjusted with a tenacity and resilience that is truly admirable, an outstanding example of America's pioneering nature.

Our look at Vermont in *Green Mountain Rails* is that of the post-World War II period when amateur photographers discovered color film. Although the photographic essay contained here spans nearly 50 years, the emphasis is on the rail picture circa 1950, when steam operation was still prevalent. We are fortunate to have many color slides from the late 1940s, just as the steam engine began its retreat from the American railroad theatre. Especially rewarding are the wonderful photographs of the Rutland and Central Vermont, the state's two most important systems. Regrettably there are no steam photos for some of the roads, simply because none was found.

Diesels and their imaginative color schemes have provided another rich palette for this volume, and we sought to illustrate as many different designs as possible from the 1940s to the present. Also, each railroad was given at least one photograph from the contemporary era, usually at the close of its respective section. The geographic orientation in the first two chapters on the Rutland and Central Vermont is from north to south, while in the smaller chapters the arrangement is arbitrary. Also arbitrary was the author's decision to include the entire Central Vermont, even though two-fifths of it are in Massachusetts and Connecticut, in part because so much excellent photography was available. The map on the front end paper should give a clear idea of where each line was located, its size and endpoints.

The narratives are brief and are intended to provide the reader with salient information about the origins of each road. Those systems covered in Chapter VI, "City Cousins," contain history relating only to their appearance in Vermont. For the more curious reader, the bibliography lists a number of fine books replete with myriad detail of Vermont's rail system. Especially laudable is the 1993 publication *Railroads of Vermont* (two volumes) by Robert C. Jones, a very comprehensive look at its subject.

My own initiation to the Rutland happened when my Dad took my brother and me to Rutland, Vermont, on a fall Saturday in 1961. On the way we passed through Bellows Falls, where, along the riverbank, there was a string of idle yellow and green boxcars labeled "Rutland." Now that was indeed a revelation. I had assumed for years that the Rutland was a railroad in Virginia, because my aunt Ann was from Rutland, Virginia. I never imagined it was in Vermont. It was many years later, after reading Jim Shaughnessy's *The Rutland Road*, that it came to me that those boxcars were there because of the now infamous strike which killed the railroad. At Chester we zoomed passed a most wonderful looking brick depot, which it took me all of 25 years to revisit. All the way up to Rutland we passed railroad tracks, bridges, and railroad paraphernalia, but no trains, alas.

So, good friends, welcome to an illustration of an era which has passed. Railroads grow and change in their lives, like all living things. They adapt to survive in the present, and Vermont's railroads today are quite another phenomenon than what they were after World War II. America came to realize very quickly then that it wanted to stretch its legs and strike out anew. Railroad domination had noticeably begun to fade in the 1920s, but it wasn't until the late 1940s that our citizens flocked to the highways in enormous numbers. In a few more short years the Interstate Highway system would throttle the railroads and all but do them in. The brave, new railroads we know today have emerged as a matter of practicality and the relentless bottom line of the balance sheet, and they are of this time and place. Life is, after all, ephemeral.

For those of us inclined to nostalgia, perhaps the saddest loss is that of the vast human network once in place to operate America's rails, a system that carried America through the Industrial Revolution. Frequently the lives of an entire family revolved around the railroad. And surely in Vermont, where railroading was such an intensely personal profession because of the state's rural make-up, the loss is felt even more keenly.

Now we have grown up and an era has slipped by, imperceptibly when measured by moments, cataclysmically when measured by decades. We remember it fondly, we treasure its images, we honor its values. We can surely profit by discerning its commendable attributes and employ them in building for the future.

Robert Willoughby Jones
Silverlake
Los Angeles, California
January 1994

A brakeman with a smile and a wave, aboard Grand Trunk 0-6-0 No. 7530, works the Island Pond yard in July 1954. Arthur E. Mitchell photo.

Introduction

I

RUTLAND

Vermont Railway • Green Mountain Railroad

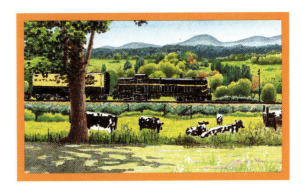

The Green Mountains were a challenge to Vermonters from the beginning. The ridge extending down the middle of the state formed a barrier that everyone had to reckon with. It was an obstruction to commerce, a hindrance to communication, a formidable obstacle to the gregarious. The mountains had to be crossed and climbed. The wily rivers flushing the steep flanks had to be tamed; forests skidded out of the hills; intractable snows navigated in winter; barns and homesteads had to be fixed on the rocky slopes. The barrier was an eternal dare; it gave year-round battle. And the mountains would have won if the first combatants hadn't possessed the ingenuity and tenacity to master them.

W. Storrs Lee
The Green Mountains of Vermont

Looking back with nostalgia on the Rutland, Vermont's railroad jewel, from the perspective of three decades after a decisive strike closed it in 1961, we may be surprised that it once comprised some 278 miles. Though a marginal operation at the time of its demise, the Rutland once stretched from Bellows Falls, Vermont, to Ogdensburg, New York, carrying a magnitude of freight traffic to and from the Great Lakes. The Rutland's heyday lay in the scant 14 years from 1901 to 1915, from its acquisition of the Ogdensburg & Lake Champlain, up until the passage of the Panama Canal Act which outlawed the road's ownership of its own lake transit company.

Success on the Rutland was always a sometimes thing. Milk, its last truly lucrative commodity, was seriously reduced in 1958 when a federal marketing order completely eliminated its New York outlet. Trucking proved to be a more efficient way of shipping milk, and the rest of this trade slipped away fast.

The two railroads we know as the Rutland and the Central Vermont were chartered simultaneously in 1843 with virtual duplicate end points. While they spent their first five decades engaged in a nasty fight, in wasteful competition, their fates today are vastly different than their inter-married, and at one time much larger cousin, the Boston & Maine. For where vast mileage of the B&M empire has long since disappeared, much original Rutland and Central Vermont trackage operates today, albeit the former under different corporate structures.

Vermont rail enthusiasts like to revel in the fascination of the sometimes quaint trains in this countryside landscape, but it is useful to remember that railroads were spawned from the profit motive. Individuals with capital to invest often believed there were fortunes to be made in railroads. Some succeeded.

Rail Beginnings in Vermont

Vermont's need for better transportation became acute with the first large influx of settlers following the War of 1812. There was good farm land in the valleys producing rich yields, and an abundance of timber, iron ore, and marble elsewhere in the state, with no efficient way of

The Green Mountain Flyer has just crossed Brooksville Bridge, north of Middlebury, on its daily northbound run to Montreal on April 20, 1952. John Gardner photo.

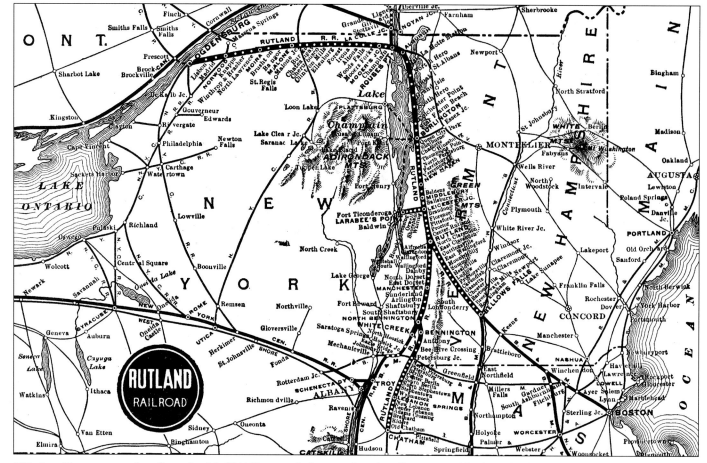

This timetable map excerpt from September 24, 1944 illustrates the large number of small towns served by the Rutland. RWJ collection.

exporting these products. The lucrative Boston market seemed unattainable. While water traffic on the Great Lakes boomed, the natural, burning entrepreneurial question was how to join Boston and the Great Lakes. A number of efforts to join them by canal failed in the planning stages because no one dared risk capital against the seemingly insurmountable engineering difficulties of crossing the Green Mountains by water.

Railroads were quick to get the attention of Vermonters. With a mere 25 railroad miles operating in the U. S. in 1830, influential Montpelier businessmen met to consider railroad plans, proposing a 400-mile line from Ogdensburg, New York, on the St. Lawrence River, to Boston. Yet, for all the intense interest, no money was committed. Even when the first Vermont railroad charter was granted by the Assembly in 1831, for a line to go west from Rutland to New York's Great Northern Canal at the head of Lake Champlain at Whitehall, no work was done.

As railroad lines were built in other states in the next decade, Vermonters became increasingly interested in following suit. They eyed with envy the progress of the Fitchburg, Boston & Lowell, Northern of New Hampshire, and Northern of New York Railroads.

The Vermont Assembly, reacting to strong demands from rival business interests, tried to please them all by granting *four* separate railroad charters in 1843:

• Connecticut & Passumpsic Rivers Railroad, from the Connecticut River Valley to Canada.

• Vermont & Massachusetts Railroad, from Brattleboro to Fitchburg.

• Champlain & Connecticut River Railroad, from Burlington to the Connecticut River Valley.

• Vermont Central Railroad, from Burlington to the Connecticut River Valley.

The last two were virtual duplicates, the first led by Judge Timothy Follett, steamboat magnate, to go via Addison, Rutland, and Windsor counties to the Connecticut River, the second led by Governor Charles Paine to go via the White and Onion River Valleys, and Northfield, his home town. Judge Follett won the support of Rutland businessmen, so naturally his road would serve this city. Thus began a wasteful rivalry which would fester off and on for half a century.

Judge Follett's organization was soon re-chartered as the Rutland & Burlington. Despite Governor Paine's active interference, some 94 miles of the R&B were completed by January 1849 between Burlington and Rutland, and between Ludlow and Bellows Falls, with a 25-mile gap.

A new player emerged when St. Albans banker John Smith chartered his Vermont & Canada Railroad from Highgate to a junction with the Vermont Central and the R&B at a "convenient" place in Chittendon County. In the end, Smith favored the VC and denied interchange to the R&B, thwarting any northern interchange.

Right: After the end of Rutland passenger service in 1953, the "Alburg & Bos." RPO stamp was still used on B&M mail cars between Bellows Falls and Boston. Howard F. Moulton collection.

Above: Rutland 403, an Alco RS-1, is working the local freight at Rouses Point, New York, in August 1955. Allan W. Styffe photo.

Right: The Alburgh station housed not only Rutland railroad offices, but also the Railway Express Agency, the town clerk, the U. S. Customs office, and "Pearl's Department Stores." Arthur E. Mitchell photo from the summer of 1953.

Below: This bright, cold February 23, 1952, a local freight is at Alburgh. John Gardner photo.

Still, in December 1849 the first two R&B trains rolled from Rutland and Bellows Falls to a rock cut at the summit, where there was much speech- and merrymaking. Expenses had been unexpectedly high and revenues were below projections, in part because of the failure to connect with the V&C. Yet the line was completed, and represented the first leg in the eventual Rutland system.

Expanding the Railroad

The road's second leg was created in 1853 with the completion of rails between Rutland and Troy, New York, over two roads: Western Vermont, from Rutland to White Creek, New York, via North Bennington; and the Troy & Boston, from White Creek to Troy. Immediately the R&B's fortunes rose nicely with the added traffic. Subsequently the combination of the Rutland & Whitehall and the Saratoga & Washington provided an interchange to the west. These two rail avenues, plus a modest amount of steamboat traffic on Lake Champlain, helped to keep the R&B alive. In 1865 the Western Vermont was renamed the Bennington & Rutland.

Through east-west freight traffic travelled circuitously on the R&B (from Bellows Falls to Rutland, while the B&R took over from Rutland to White Creek) from 1852 until 1875 when the long-awaited Hoosac Tunnel finally opened. Since only 52 miles were on the R&B, profits were thin and the R&B had difficulty meeting its debt.

Governor Paine lost control of the Vermont Central in 1852 to John Smith, who now held both the Vermont Central and the Vermont & Canada. Smith was no more sympathetic to the R&B than Paine in effecting a northern interchange.

In February 1854 the R&B defaulted on both its first- and second-mortgage bonds, and was forced to float a third mortgage for $1,200,000 for operating cash. A struggle among Boston investors holding the first- and second-mortgage certificates nearly froze operations. By 1855 only a single mixed train managed a daily round trip between Rutland and Bellows Falls. Finally in October the mortgage holders declared peace just to keep the tattered road operating.

The battle for a connection with the Vermont Central was finally won in 1860. Trustee John B. Page took control, bringing new inspiration to the tired little road and its beleaguered operating people. In 1867 the road was reorganized as the Rutland Railroad, and now-President Page also became Governor of Vermont. Page and his board took decisive action which not only freed the Rutland from dependence on the Vermont Central, but which also positioned it to capture significant overhead traffic. Most important was the leasing of the Vermont Valley and Vermont & Massachusetts Railroads, providing interchange with the New London Northern at Millers Falls, Massachusetts. The Vermont Central, panicked over its evaporating advantage, signed a 20-year lease with the Rutland to cap its growth.

This is the left half of the Cash Fare Receipt which the conductor of the train was required to submit to the Rutland comptroller's office for audit. The two forms were mirror images of each other so that the conductor had only to make one set of punches for each transaction. Because this side was not given to passengers, examples are very rare. Note that both Ogdensburg and Chatham lines are shown. Jack May collection.

The new Vermont Central

Vermont Central's 793 resulting track miles and two steamship lines gave it complete control from New London to Ogdensburg by rail, and from there across the Great Lakes by water. It was through the Rutland-controlled Vermont Valley and Vermont & Massachusetts that the VC gained access to New London, Connecticut. Yet the deal was less advantageous than hoped. By taking traffic away from the Rutland, the VC in effect reduced its own revenues.

The 1873 post-war recession caused the road to reorganize as the Central Vermont Railroad. By 1875 it was $282,000 in arrears in Rutland lease payments. It dumped Rutland-acquired leases of the Whitehall & Plattsburgh and Montreal & Plattsburgh Railroads, and of the steamboat *Oakes Ames*, and took on instead the Harlem Extension Railroad (the old Western Vermont or Bennington & Rutland, and the Lebanon Springs), forming a circuitous route to New York.

On the horizon was the threat of the rapidly growing Delaware & Hudson. When the Rutland lease was up in 1890, the CV leased it for another 99 years to keep it from direct D&H control. Even so the D&H actually dominated the Rutland Board. Unfortunately depression struck hard in 1893, and three years later the CV went into receivership, abrogating its Rutland lease. Then in 1898 an anxious D&H sold its Rutland stock, grateful to be rid of its questionable investment.

Reaching West and South

Free of D&H control, the Rutland owners concentrated on upgrading track and equipment. By 1899 the Rutland redoubled its efforts to pursue St. Lawrence to Boston traffic as well as that from Canada to New York City.

On the north, the Rutland absorbed the Ogdensburg & Lake Champlain on September 27, 1901, cementing control of its own route to the Great Lakes. To provide its own link between Burlington and the end of the Ogdensburg line at Rouses Point—and cast off its lingering dependency on the CV—the Rutland built the Rutland & Canadian from Burlington to Rouses Point, New York. This 40-mile extension began on a three-mile, marble-rip-rapped causeway to South Hero Island, and stretched across Grand Isle and North Hero Island to Alburgh, then crossing Lake Champlain to Rouses Point.

This last acquisition began as the Northern Railroad of New York, completed between Rouses Point and Ogdensburg in September 1850. In 1858 the road was reorganized into the Ogdensburg Railroad, then in 1864 into the Ogdensburg & Lake Champlain. The Vermont Central leased it in March 1870 for 20 years, along with its increasingly lucrative boat operation, the Ogdensburg Transportation Company. After the CV defaulted on interest payments in 1896, the O&LC was purchased in

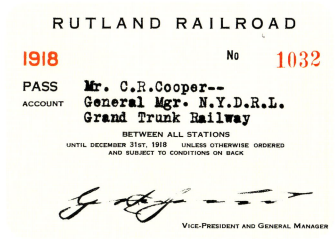

Top: We're at North Hero Station in June 1951. John Gardner photo.

Above: A Rutland Railroad employee pass from 1918. RWJ collection.

Rutland 17

18   Green Mountain Rails

Above Left: *This is the fill seen from South Hero Island, with New York's magnificent Adirondacks in the distance. Imagine riding this route on such a fine day as this, in the fall of 1964.* **Below left:** *The photographer hiked a ways out on the fill to make these two shots in June 1951. Pacific 84 is southbound, while Pacific 83,* **above**, *is northbound.* **Below:** *Here's the Green Mountain Flyer northbound at Colchester, just about to enter the three-mile fill to South Hero Island. Four photos by John Gardner.*

Rutland 19

1901 by the Rutland, whose managers diligently increased business and improved the physical plant.

In 1875 the New York & Canada had been completed from Whitehall to Rouses Point, completing the Delaware & Hudson trunk line. Lucrative coal from Pennsylvania was then routed via Rouses Point to water navigation at Ogdensburg.

The Rutland now controlled 278 miles of mainline. Combined with the Fitchburg Railroad connection, it had a trunk route 392 miles from Boston to Ogdensburg, then by boat to Chicago and Duluth.

To the south, the Rutland bought two contiguous lines to give it direct interchange at Chatham, New York, with the New York & Harlem and the Boston & Albany. The Bennington & Rutland was acquired in 1900, the Chatham and Lebanon Valley in 1901—the latter having a complex history. The two roads once formed what promoters hoped would be a competitive New York-Montreal route. From 1872 to 1877 they were controlled by the Central Vermont.

In 1869 the B&R arranged financing to complete the Lebanon Springs Railroad (later the C&LV) to Bennington so that the B&R could complete the route from Chatham to Rutland. Always a financial quagmire—the line never had much revenue—it had several corporate names and owners. The recurrent failures of the Lebanon Springs were the result of chronic low revenues. The Rutland fared better than its predecessors and long operated an Ogdensburg-Chatham milk train. The nick-name "Corkscrew Division" derived from the trackage in Vermont laid in a squiggly manner in hilly country. Not only was it considerably longer than its rivals, but much slower as well. The Rutland expended a lot of money in the early 1900s to bring the line up to company operating standards.

New Directions

In its status as a newly profitable system, the Rutland attracted the attention of the New York Central & Hudson River Railroad and Dr. William Seward Webb, son-in-law of William H. Vanderbuilt. When Webb's gubernatorial ambitions in New York were thwarted, he looked to Vermont and the Rutland where he and the NYC&HR owned more than half the corporate stock. Operation under this benevolent parentage was smooth and profitable, and much enjoyed by the minority stockholders. He never achieved the governorship, though.

The New Haven Railroad, which considered New England its exclusive domain, became alarmed at this NYC&HR intrusion in Vermont, and as a protective measure bought control of the New York, Ontario & Western. A swap was considered to settle the difficulty, though the solution embraced in 1911 allowed the New Haven to purchase one half the Central's interest in the Rutland. Minority stockholder opposition prolonged litigation until 1915.

The lucrative freight transfer at Ogdensburg, which brought prosperity to the Rutland, was stopped cold by the Panama Canal Act of 1915. It amended the Interstate Commerce Act to forbid a railroad from owning a competing interstate water carrier. Predictably, the New York Central got all the business.

Still, wartime traffic increases kept the Rutland busy, and indeed the railroad was virtually consumed under the control of the United States Railway Administration, which managed maximum wartime traffic with minimum maintenance. Postwar passenger traffic increased until 1924 when the meteoric rise of the automobile eroded business quickly. Although the milk trade was still increasing, the road had seen its best and prosperous days. As resourceful as the Rutland tried to be, it would never again regain its recent prosperity.

Passenger trains on the Chatham division, never profitable, were eliminated in favor of busses in 1926; these lasted five years.

The November 1927 flooding caused 356 washouts costing $1 million. Miraculously, the railroad was down for only two weeks; the Central Vermont was unable to open its mainline until the following February.

Revenues dropped drastically between 1929 and 1937, from $6,276,682 to $3,483,634. Unable to meet bond payments in 1938, the Rutland went into receivership. The road took significant steps to economize while operating, including wage cuts, major tax reductions from both New York and Vermont, the creation of the booster-like "Save the Rutland Club," and a new, faster freight train between Bellows Falls and Norwood, New York, called "The Whippet," including a reconditioned but tired 1913-vintage 2-8-0 freshly tarted up in black and silver.

Between 1941 and 1950 there were several attempts at codifying a reorganization plan, all the while various bond- and shareholder groups sought payment, and employees—spurred by national unions—sought raises and payment of deferred wages. The most novel of the plans would have reformed the railroad to resemble a farm cooperative, an idea with creative merit if not much political practicality.

November 1950 saw the formation of a new company, the Rutland Rail*way*, with major bondholder Gardner Caverly as chairman of the management committee. Caverly applied the pruning knife with a firm hand, scrapping unproductive branches and sidings, including the albatross "Corkscrew" division to Chatham which had generated virtually no on-line freight revenue whatever in its 94-year life. Fifteen new diesels replaced 58 steam locomotives, and a new fleet of freight cars com-

Opposite above left and right: *Seen from a bridge spanning the tracks, a northbound freight departs the north end of Burlington in February 1951.*

Right: *The same day another freight is headed north out of Burlington. Three photos by John Gardner.*

Above: Rutland 0-6-0 No. 107 is working near the coaling tower at Burlington on August 19, 1952. Stephen R. Payne photo.

Above: Rutland's four Mountains had beautiful lines indeed. When delivered in 1946 they were painted green, and employees were soon calling them "Green Hornets." Later, practical considerations—two men needed two days to do the job—caused them to be painted in the more conventional black in 1948. Here No. 92 is checked over by the hogger in July 1951.

Right: RS-3 205 appears to be right-out-of-the-box on August 23 1952. She's northbound at Burlington with a milk train. Two photos by John Gardner.

prised 450 boxcars, 70 gondolas, and 27 hoppers.

The $400,000 annual loss from passenger service was solved easily in 1953 when a short strike closed the line. The railroad simply never operated any more passenger trains, even over the protests of the Vermont Public Service Commission.

Management modernized the physical plant, bought new maintenance-of-way equipment, closed stations, consolidated agencies, and cut the staff in half. The passenger station in Rutland was sadly replaced by a parking lot, and the old coach shop was converted for a headquarters building.

The long-idle Ogdensburg grain elevator went into use again in 1955 when the U. S. began a grain storage project. As operation in the fifties became efficient and prosperous, there was optimism that the railroad was doing well. There was even a dividend paid on preferred stock in 1957. This rosy picture was accomplished with the willing help of labor, who had foregone raises and whose rates had fallen behind the national norm.

Then, in the late fifties, revenue began a decline, especially in the critical milk trade. William I. Ginsberg bought the railroad in 1957 and attempted to adjust operating practices to reflect the level of traffic—by reducing the three operating subdivisions to two. The employees struck in September 1960. They neither liked nor trusted Ginsberg.

The walkout was stopped after 41 days by Federal injunction, followed by a one-year cooling off period. Lamentably, negotiations all year found both management and labor intransigent, and the strike resumed September 25, 1961. Determined to yield at least some value for stockholders, Ginsberg filed for abandonment in December. This too was vigorously fought by labor, but a year later it was mercifully approved, with Vermont purchasing two key portions of right-of-way: Burlington-White Creek, New York, and Rutland-Bellows Falls. Except for the western-most piece in New York, acquired by the Ogdensburg Bridge & Port Authority, the rest of the Ogdensburg division was ripped up for salvage.

Vermont Railway

In mid-1963 the state found a new operator in Jay Wulfson, of the Middletown & New Jersey Railroad, who started the Vermont Railway. The newly-formed road took over operation of the 131 miles from Burlington to White Creek and Bennington, commencing business in January 1964. The new image included a bright red and white paint scheme with a modern, mountain-inspired logo. The new road, with its short-line labor rules, has been successful from the start, and today enjoys profitable levels of freight. Incoming products include dairy feed, fertilizers, agricultural products, fuel oil, coal, gasolene, road salt, propane, and lumber. Outgoing are marble and marble chips, forest products, paper, and various manufactured goods—occasionally including maple syrup. The Vermont Railway bought the Clarendon & Pittsford in 1972 from the Vermont Marble Co. (see chapter V).

Innovations in the 1970s included the addition of 5,000 piggyback trailers, 950 boxcars, and the inauguration of a tank car train in 1978. In 1981 the VTR leased the five miles of track from White Creek to Hoosick Junction, New York, from parent Boston & Maine after it failed to provide adequate upkeep. Subsidiary Clarendon & Pittsford purchased the 24 miles of track from Rutland to Whitehall, New York, in 1983 from the Delaware & Hudson, quickly beginning track rehabilitation. Today this line sees six-day-a-week operation of VTR's largest regularly scheduled freight.

The VTR's financial picture has been impressive, with revenues increasing from $539,000 to $3 million between 1964 and 1985. Success of the company can be attributed to a can-do spirit, coupled with a lean physical plant, a small and versatile work force, and personalized service.

Green Mountain Railroad

The other leg of the Rutland to be preserved, from Bellows Falls to Rutland, was reactivated first by Nelson Blount and his Steamtown tourist operation in 1964. As an outgrowth of this he began the Green Mountain Railroad, and it began carrying freight in April 1965. Originally Blount proposed to lease tracks only as far as Ludlow, but he was persuaded of the advantages of going to Rutland and having interchange at either end.

Business improved markedly in 1967 when the Boston & Maine began to cooperate by interchanging freight at Bellows Falls. This was due in part to GMRC's willingness to accommodate long B&M freights after a major wreck closed the Hoosac Tunnel for eight days in February 1967.

Just as the Rutland painfully learned how devastating New England storms can be, the Green Mountain has suffered similarly. Serious rains and flooding in 1973, 1975, 1976, and 1984 closed the road for weeks at a time.

Passenger trains have become a very popular summer attraction. This service, originally offered by Green Mountain, was turned over to Steamtown in 1970. When Steamtown left for Scranton, Pennsylvania, in 1983, the newly-formed Vermont Historical Railroad, Inc. ran trains in the summer of 1984 with mixed success. Green Mountain resumed responsibility for operating the trains for the historical group the following summer, and clever marketing has effected ridership increases ever since.

Freight revenues have fluctuated dramatically since 1965, with several low periods followed with impressive increases. In recent years significant business has resulted from considerable bridge traffic, northbound with fly ash and southbound with limestone slurry.

The Green Mountain became 49% employee-owned following Nelson Blount's death, and today has forged success through hard work and caring service.

Both of these new roads honor the stick-to-it tradition fostered by the Rutland in the Green Mountain state.

Left: *A lone Rutland caboose stands between the Burlington turntable and the blue waters of Lake Champlain on October 18, 1953.*

Below left: *Here's a nice portrait of 107, an 0-6-0 switcher, in February 1951 in the Burlington Yard. The locomotive was purchased from the Clarendon & Pittsford for $500 in 1946 when that road dieselized.*

Right: *Dramatic back-lighting silhouettes a double-headed freight northbound out of Burlington in June 1951.*

Below right: *Northbound, north of Burlington, RS-3 201 is headed into some pretty fall foliage in September 1956. Four photos by John Gardner.*

24   Green Mountain Rails

Above left: *Winter is still in evidence this April 18, 1952, as Pacific 85 hauls a train across the Shelburne embankment with three head-end cars and a coach.*
Stephen R. Payne photo.

Left: *The southbound Green Mountain Flyer is blowing up snow as she heads through Shelburne on February 22, 1952.*

Above: *It's late on an autumn afternoon in 1950 as Ten-Wheeler No. 52 pulls north through Vergennes. She would be scrapped a year later. Two photos by John Gardner.*

Right: *The charming brick depot at New Haven was photographed in the fall of 1954 by Arthur E. Mitchell.*

Below: *Rutland Railroad ticket, Burlington and Vergennes. Jack May collection.*

Left: *A northbound freight behind Ten-Wheeler 52 is dramatically lighted by the late afternoon sun at Middlebury in January 1951. John Gardner photo.*

Below: *The hogger checks his engine, 4-6-2 No 80, as express is unloaded at Middlebury in June 1948. Looks like the milk business is good. Norton D. Clark collection.*

Right: *RS-1 405 has a freight at Leicester Junction on April 17, 1952. In earlier days on the Rutland, trains could travel on the Addison Branch from here across Lake Champlain to Fort Ticonderoga via the notorious floating bridge.*

Below right: *This is the graceful covered bridge at Shoreham on the Addison Branch in January 1951. The branch was abandoned On May 21 the same year. Two photos by John Gardner.*

28   Green Mountain Rails

Rutland 29

Above: Rutland 4-6-2 No. 85 has the Green Mountain Flyer at Pittsford on August 13, 1952. The train carries a milk car, two express cars, a B&M "American Flyer" coach, and a combine in a fresh Rutland paint scheme. Stephen R. Payne photo. *Below:* The beautiful Proctor depot, seen here in October 1958, was the site of terrible flooding in 1927. Proctor was also served by the Clarendon & Pittsford (p.132). Arthur E.

PASSENGER SERVICE ON THE RUTLAND

For a railroad running through a sparsely populated area, especially the line to Ogdensburg, the Rutland operated a tenacious passenger service. The famed *White Mountain Express* made its way from Niagara to Portland, Maine, via the Rutland's upper arm in 24 hours in 1886, carrying a baggage car, smoker, and 9 sleepers. In those times before dining cars, meals were served at station restaurants—very quickly.

The Boston to Ogdensburg sleeping car lasted from 1901 to 1940, just before the onset of World War II. Sleeper service was then cut back to Alburgh, operating through the summer of 1947. A through coach from Boston to Ogdensburg could still be found in the summer of 1948. When, subsequently, the through connection was dropped, it was replaced with a not-so-convenient Alburgh-Ogdensburg coach on the mixed train. By this time a Boston to Ogdensburg ride was quite an ordeal. An intrepid rider left Boston at 6:45 p.m. on a coach and arrived at Rutland at 12:30 a.m., waiting there until 6:30 a.m. when a local train left for Ogdensburg where it would arrive at 4:00 p.m. Returning, one left Ogdensburg at 7:30 a.m., arriving Rutland at 4:40 p.m., in time for dinner, a movie, and perhaps a dime novel until the 2:30 a.m. departure. Arrival in Boston was a 9:00 a.m. when you might be less than fresh.

Here's what was listed in the road's final passenger timetable on April 26, 1953—service which all ended later in the summer with the strike:

Mount Royal—NY-Montreal daily sleeping cars and coaches, 9:45 p.m.-9:00 a.m. Northbound, a coach connection from Boston required a four-hour layover at Rutland.

Green Mountain—NY-Burlington daily coach (diner for Albany for lunch northbound, diner from Troy for dinner southbound), 11:30 a.m.-8:00 p.m. Sandwiches between Rutland and Burlington. Coach connection from Boston, to Burlington and Ogdensburg via milk train.

Milk Train—Rutland-Alburgh, 1:35 p.m.-5:00 p.m. northbound; 11:50 a.m. (from Rouses Point)-3:35 p.m. southbound.

Mixed Train—Alburgh-Ogdensburg

Both Rutland-Boston segments of the *Green Mountain* and the *Mount Royal* also connected at Bellows Falls with Connecticut River trains.

This June 23, 1935, 20-page timetable was an elaborate affair. Prominent ads featured the Green Mountain Flyer, *the* Mount Royal, *freight connections, industrial opportunities, and bus tours from Rutland. Conway Scenic Railway collection.*

Rutland 31

Above left: B&M Pacific 3708 blasts out of Rutland past the ball signal with the Boston section of the *Green Mountain Flyer* in April 1952. David C. Bartlett photo.

Left: A big disappointment to the photographer, an inveterate steam afficionado, was RS-3 204 on the point of this train near Rutland on August 13, 1952. Reportedly Pacific 83 had encountered operating difficulties. Stephen R. Payne photo.

Above right: The Rutland engine facility on August 8, 1950 was a very busy place. In the center a double-headed freight is departing for the south. The passenger station is at the very far right. David C. Bartlett photo.

Right: The beautifully proportioned Mountain, No. 93, enters Rutland with an express and passenger train on April 9, 1952. Stephen R. Payne photo.

Rutland 33

34 Green Mountain Rails

Left: Ten-Wheeler No. 74 is pulling away from a passenger train on September 22, 1951. The Rutland depot is in the background. Note the awnings on the windows.

Below left: The crew of Rutland's Mountain No. 93 has just stepped down for a coffee break. We're at Rutland on September 22, 1951. Two photos by Russell F. Munroe.

Above right: Two freshly painted Rutland cabooses on November 12, 1951. John Gardner photo.

Center right: The photographer was on his honeymoon when he made this photo in Rutland on June 22, 1958. Note that the cupola is dark green while the main body color is black. John F. Kane photo.

Below right: A close-up detail of an old wooden Rutland boxcar. John Gardner photo.

Below: Rutland Railroad strip ticket, punched October 31, 1943, Burlington-Rouses Point-Montreal. Jack May collection.

Rutland

Left: *Alco RS-3 201 shunts a milk car at Rutland on September 22, 1951. Russell F. Munroe photo.*

Below: *Rutland Railroad ticket, Brandon and Rutland. Jack May collection.*

Bottom: *On April 9, 1952, 0-6-0 No. 100 works the yard at Rutland. Stephen R. Payne photo.*

Above: Rutland 4-6-2 No. 82 enters Rutland with baggage and mail on September 22, 1951. The third car is an unusual RPO-coach combination. Russell F. Munroe photo.

Below: RS-3s 208 and 204 in front of the Rutland engine house on June 22, 1958. John F. Kane photo.

38   Green Mountain Rails

Above Left: *The Green Mountain Flyer is on the curve at East Clarendon behind Pacific 82 on January 22, 1951. Stephen R. Payne photo.* **Below left:** *A double-headed freight behind Mikado 35 on a beautiful August day in 1950, at the same location. David C. Bartlett photo.* **Above:** *Looking south from the rear passenger platform in January 1951, south of Rutland.* **Below:** *Aboard Rutland JX2 somewhere between Burlington and Rutland on August 8, 1959. Two photos by John Gardner.*

Left: *A pair of Rutland Mikados, Nos. 35 and 34, on Cuttingsville Trestle on August 8, 1950.*

Bottom: *One of four Rutland Mountains, No. 91, with the* Green Mountain Flyer *at Chester on February 6, 1951.*

Right: *The late afternoon winter sun shines amber on Consolidation 27 at Mt. Holly on January 22, 1951.*

Below right: *4-6-2 No. 80 is crossing a snow-laden field near Chester on February 2, 1951. The first and third cars are from the B&M. Four photos by Stephen R. Payne.*

Below: *Rutland Railroad ticket, Cavendish and Ludlow. Jack May collection.*

40   Green Mountain Rails

Above: On a bright and wintry February 2, 1951, Ten-Wheeler 79 rushes through the bridge at Rockingham. Stephen R. Payne photo. *Below:* This official company photo of RS-3 205 southbound at the Bartonsville covered bridge was made famous in the first edition of Jim Shaughnessy's The Rutland Road. Jim Shaughnessy collection.

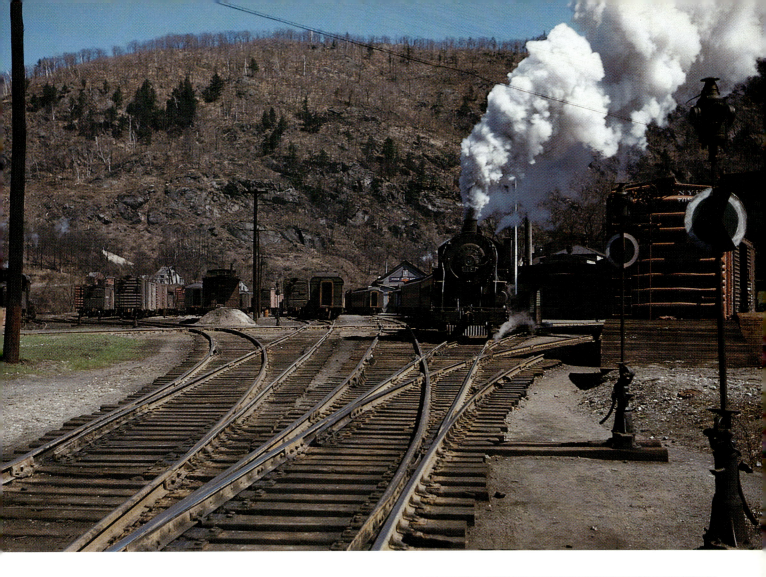

Above: The Green Mountain Flyer *pulls out of Bellows Falls behind Pacific 75 for Rutland with a full head of steam in this undated winter view. The minimal real estate here made it necessary for no fewer than four diamonds in crossing the B&M mainline. Leon Onofri photo.*

Right: According to the photographer, January 9, 1951 was one of the coldest days he ever experienced in making railroad photos. 4-6-0 No. 79 is at Bellows Falls. Stephen R. Payne photo.

Rutland 43

44   Green Mountain Rails

Left: *Rutland Mountain 93 pulls into the Bellows Falls yard across the B&M mainline on August 9, 1952. Norton D. Clark collection.*

Below left: *Rutland's Consolidation 29 at the Bellows Falls roundhouse on July 31, 1950. Stephen R. Payne photo.*

*Rutland switcher No. 106 was an 0-6-0 built by Alco at Schenectady in 1914 and retired in September 1953. The loco was outshopped just before these photos were made. Stephen R. Payne made these studies, **right** and **center right**, of 0-6-0 No. 106 on the Bellows Falls turntable on August 13, 1952.*

Below right: *An attentive crewman oils No. 106 adjacent to the Bellows Falls water and coaling facilities in the summer of 1952. Arthur E. Mitchell photo.*

Below: *Rutland Railway tickets, Bellows Falls and Rutland, and Ogdensburg to Madrid, New York. Jack May collection.*

Rutland 45

Right: *Two proud Rutland beauties: Pacific 83 on the left; Mountain 93 on the right, on a hot August 9, 1952. Norton D. Clark collection.*

Below right: *Immaculately painted 0-6-0 No. 106 is switching some local freight business across the stone arch bridge on the Connecticut River in summer 1953 from North Walpole, New Hampshire, to Bellows Falls. Note the brakeman riding the side of the NYC box car. Arthur E. Mitchell photo.*

Above: *The joint B&M-Rutland freight house was a longtime fixture at Bellows Falls.* **Below:** *We're looking west from the Bellows Falls depot as the Rutland main line crosses the girder bridge. The operator who controls the ball signal is having a midday chat with the station agent. Two photos by Arthur E. Mitchell from the summer of 1953.*

46   Green Mountain Rails

On a sun-drenched August 8, 1950, Mountain 92 is southbound with the Green Mountain Flyer at Clarendon. Stephen R. Payne photo.

RPO indicia from the Alburgh & Troy route. Courtesy of Howard T. Moulton.

Here are three picturesque Rutland depots photographed by Arthur E. Mitchell on the line between Rutland and Bennington.

Above Right: The Wallingford depot possessed a classic simplicity. It is unusual to find a bay window on the end of a depot, rather than on the front. Photographed in 1952.

Right: The lush summer greenery is resplendent at Manchester in 1960.

Below right: The Arlington Depot in summer 1960.

Rutland 49

Left: Ten-Wheeler 74 pulls into North Bennington on August 14, 1952 with a local freight.

Below: The same train is viewed from a different angle. North Bennington depot, in use today as an architect's office, was one of the most stately to be built on the Rutland. Standing adjacent was the once ubiquitous ball signal, and a wooden milk car.

Right: The conductor prepares to descend at North Bennington upon the arrival of his local freight. The train will interchange with the B&M freight waiting at right. January 5, 1951.

Below right: The richness of summer is captured in this shot of 4-6-0 No. 40 at Bennington on August 8, 1950. Bennington became the end of track after the Corkscrew Division was ripped up in 1953. Four photos by Stephen R. Payne.

50   Green Mountain Rails

Rutland 51

Above: On a still-wintry April 12, 1952, Stephen R. Payne found 4-6-0 No. 76 on the Armstrong turntable at Bennington.
Below: Here is another view of No. 40 at Bennington on August 8, 1950. Two photos by Stephen R. Payne.

52   Green Mountain Rails

Above: *The conductor is riding the back platform at Bennington this beautiful August 14, 1952.*
Below: *It's January 2, 1951, just two years before the demise of the Corkscrew Division, and Mikado 32 pulls into Chatham, New York, with a southbound freight. This is the only color photo of the Rutland in Chatham found for this book. Two photos by Stephen R. Payne.*

VERMONT RAILWAY

54   Green Mountain Rails

Here is a brief look at Vermont Railway operations, in the vibrant and highly visible red scheme with the white mountain logo.

Left: A Vermont Railway local has just passed the old brick North Bennington Depot in February 1991. VTR GP-38-2 202 and Clarendon & Pittsford GP-9 752 make up the power today. Mike Confalone photo.

Below left: Here's C&P 752 on a VTR freight—eastbound on the Waloomsac, New York, bridge—on its way from Hoosick Junction to North Bennington, two days after Christmas in 1988. The 752 later went to the Black River & Western.

Right: A Bennington-bound freight passes the Common and Post Office at Danby on February 28, 1969 behind RS-1 404.

Below: VTR GP-38-2 201 on the point of BR-2 is battling drifting snow at Shelburne on February 13, 1988. Three photos by Jim Shaughnessy.

Rutland 55

GREEN MOUNTAIN RAILROAD

56 Green Mountain Rails

Left: A Green Mountain fall foliage extra at Gassetts in October 1991. At left is an old talc mill. Mike Confalone photo. **Below left:** A GMRC passenger extra behind RS-1s 400 and 401 along the Connecicut River at Bellows Falls on June 14, 1987. **Above:** The classic Chester depot is visited by a GMRC passenger train on June 13, 1987. Two photos by Jim Shaughnessy. **Below:** Russell F. Munroe made this fine photo of GMRC 2-6-0 No. 89 (ex Canadian National) on the Cuttingsville trestle over the Mill River. The excursion ran between Rutland and Bellows Falls on May 1, 1965.

II

CENTRAL VERMONT

The Railroads arrived in Vermont at just the right hour of the nineteenth century to allow the passengers to luxuriate in the national mood. Never before had the mountains been so sublime in their beauty—nor have they been since.... The steam cars began dropping off the first influx of sightseers in the 1850's. For years travelers and adventurers had been coming by stagecoach or on the Champlain boats; the traffic had brought lively summer trade to inns along the stage routes and holiday groups to the lakes, but the mountains drew the train trade. The shrewd businessmen of the hill country who had previously recognized mountains as the principal obstacle to Vermont commerce now sensed their possession of an asset. Opposite the depots of alert towns gorgeous frame hotels sprang up, with filigreed piazzas looking unto the mountains, with rooms designed to contain a great volume of mountain air, and dining service guaranteed to challenge any digestive capacity. Wicker rocking chairs were everywhere; iced cream and oysters were added to the menus.

W. Storrs Lee
The Green Mountains of Vermont

From our survey of the Rutland, it may have seemed that the Central Vermont was the proverbial big bully in its relations with its neighbor. Its indelible tenaciousness derived from its forging by Charles Paine and later through devoted nurturing by three generations of Smiths: John, his son J. Gregory, and his grandson Edward C.—all three becoming president of the railroad, and the last two serving as Governor of Vermont. The great swelling of the Vermont Central—its almost rabid overextension accomplished in a thrust at monopoly and taming the competition—was the reason for its near collapse. Its subsequent pruning down to a single mainline from Canada to Connecticut is undoubtedly responsible for the railroad's survival today. The trimming process, first begun by a financial panic in 1873, eventually allowed the Central Vermont to be a focused road with a reasonable physical plant. The codification exercise was further advanced in 1899 when the Grand Trunk Railway—having started acquiring CV stock in 1863—took control of the CV after a three-year receivership. The result was a bridge line between Lake Champlain and the Boston & Maine at White River Junction, and a budget route for goods between New York City (via New London shipping) and the west.

Today's 325-mile Central Vermont was created from four earlier roads: 1) Vermont & Canada from Rouses Point to Essex Junction; 2) Vermont Central from Burlington to Windsor; 3) Boston & Maine from Windsor to Brattleboro, and 4) New London Northern from Brattleboro to New London, Connecticut.

The Northern Division

We have already seen how the Rutland and the Vermont Central became early rivals. The CV's creator,

The elements captured in this mid-century railroad scene at Palmer, Massachusetts, are truly those of an era past. Central Vermont 2-8-0 No. 451 is flanked by a water tower, a coaling tower, and a turntable. The CV interchanged at Palmer then with the Boston & Albany—today with Conrail and Massachusetts Central. The 451 was the last CV steam engine to run— scrapped April 1957. Photographed by Stephen R. Payne on May 27, 1950.

Central Vermont 59

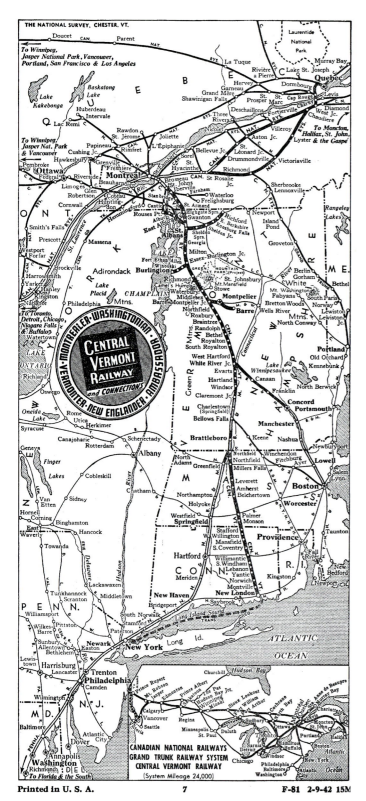

The February 9, 1942 timetable featured this system map, complete with parent Canadian National's transcontinental lines to the far west. All the mainline trains ran over the Boston & Maine's Connecticut River line south of East Northfield, Massachusetts, but the CV did operate a single daily round-trip—with a Brill car—between Brattleboro and New London. Connecting busses were provided at Essex Junction for Burlington passengers, and at Montpelier Junction for Montpelier and Barre passengers, a service which would last until November 10, 1958. RWJ collection.

Charles Paine—caught by railroad fever, and seeing a way to best the Erie Canal—obtained his first charter in November 1835 for a railroad to go from Windsor to Burlington. While his first company failed after the 1837 panic, his second attempt in 1843 moved ahead with ground-breaking in December 1845 at Windsor. Tracks from White River Junction to Bethel, 25 miles, were opened two and a half years later in June 1848. Burlington saw its first VC train on December 30, 1849. The Rutland got there first on December 18, just 13 days earlier, but there would be no spanning the three city blocks separating the two for 12 years.

Governor Paine (he served 1841-43) defied both logic and public opinion in bypassing Montpelier—not only the state's capital, but an important source of money to build the Railroad—to expedite passage of rails through Northfield, his hometown. There he profited well from selling his land to the railroad and, in the early years, by putting up guests in his hotel where trains stopped for the night. Nonetheless, the completion of the road to Burlington more than exhausted Paine's and his associates' resources; they were forced to borrow large amounts at premium interest rates.

To the north, the Vermont & Canada was being promoted by John Smith, a rich farmer from St. Albans, as a companion road to the VC. Five years after its 1845 incorporation the V&C reached 24 miles from Essex Junction on the VC to St. Albans in October 1850. By January 10, trains were running to West Alburgh, New York, where a ferry connection took passengers and goods across Lake

T. J. Donahue photographed a westbound local freight behind Grand Trunk 2611, crossing the East Alburgh trestle on a sparkling day in June 1955.

Champlain to Rouses Point. From there the Northern Railroad of New York went 118 miles west to Ogdensburg, and the Champlain & St. Lawrence went 46 miles north to Montreal. The ferry crossing was a hindrance, but marine entrepreneurs had successfully blocked the building of a bridge (earlier they had even attempted to block the V&C's chartering). A subsequent temporary solution involved a floating center span which could be moved out for passing boats, but a permanent bridge wasn't seen until 1868 when the demands of mail service caused the New York Legislature to rescind its opposition.

It was prescient John Smith who persuaded Governor Paine to accept a takeover clause in the Vermont Central's lease of the Vermont & Canada. It said that, should the VC default in its 8% annual rental of the V&C (set at $108,000 annually), the V&C would automatically take control of its parent until payments were current. A mere two years later, in 1852, the VC was in receivership and Governor Paine was out of a job (he died a year later in Waco, Texas after just a few months of promoting railroads there). Smith consolidated his position to control both roads by invoking the clause in the lease agreement. The courts upheld the position and the V&C took over the VC in July 1855. Complex legal wrangling would continue until 1861, when receivers were appointed to run the two railroads. These trustees ran them until 1873, when a reorganization resulted in a new company, the Central Vermont, taking over the Vermont Central and the Vermont & Canada.

Smith died in 1858, and was succeeded as president by his son J. Gregory Smith—another destined for the Vermont governorship (1863-64). His other son, Worthington C. Smith, became president of the Vermont & Canada. The Vermont Central grew large under J. Gregory's ambition to make the road a major player between Boston and the West. He created the Montreal & Vermont Junction Railway (St. Albans to St. Johns, Quebec) to tap lucrative shipments from Canadian ports. From its opening in January 1865 until 1946 this was the road's mainline (called the St. Armand Subdivision), after which date Montreal trains went on the Canadian National via East Alburgh and Cantic, Quebec. Smith's expansion efforts in Canada included acquisition of two smaller roads. First, the Stanstead, Sheffield & Chambly was needed for just two strategic miles and for its trestle over the Richelieu River which gave the VC access to St. Johns. To the east this 43-mile line ran through agricultural countryside to Waterloo. VC control prevented competitive use by VC's parallel rival, the Connecticut & Passumpsic Rivers Railroad. Second, the Waterloo & Magog Railroad was acquired for its eventual access to Sherbrooke in 1885. But business wasn't good and the 45 miles of leased trackage from Waterloo to Sherbrooke were relinquished in 1888. Parts of this route were later incorporated into the Canadian Pacific's line to Maine.

J. Gregory Smith finally saw the wisdom of connecting with the Rutland—after a publicly harassed railroad commissioner ordered him to do so—and ordained the building of a short branch from Winooski to Burlington which was completed in May 1861. Its 342 ft. brick-lined tunnel remains in active use today.

Central Vermont

Smith freely leased and bought unfriendly railroads—usually paying too much—whenever the profitability of his empire was threatened. To counter the burgeoning Rutland, he leased the Ogdensburg & Lake Champlain and its fleet of steamers and water terminal facilities.

To extend the Vermont Central's control south of Windsor, in 1866, Smith leased the Sullivan Railroad (owned by the Northern of New Hampshire) covering the 25 miles between Windsor and Bellows Falls. The Vermont Valley Railroad comprised the next 24 miles to Brattleboro, which the Rutland had leased a year earlier in 1865. We noted earlier how the Rutland's President Page was about to trump Smith and his recalcitrant Vermont Central by some smart connections west of Rutland, and Smith's subsequent lease of the Rutland in December 1870 to control this ambitious rival. This lease placed the Vermont Valley in Smith's control temporarily, but several later actions occurred to keep these tracks out of Central Vermont hands for over a century: 1) In April 1877 the Rutland gave up its lease of the Vermont Valley; 2) The VV bought the Sullivan County Railroad in October 1880; and 3) these two short roads, with 49 miles of track linking Windsor with Brattleboro, became part of the Connecticut River Railroad. It is puzzling how Smith let such strategic trackage slip from his control.

Yet he did act to acquire the Missisquoi Railroad in 1870, 27 miles from St. Albans to Richford, to prevent the Connecticut & Passumpsic Rivers Railroad from having entry into St. Albans. Three small railroads in New York, comprising 60 miles of track, came into the VC fold briefly, beginning in December 1870: the Whitehall and Plattsburgh; the Montreal & Plattsburgh; and the Whitehall & Plattsburgh extension to Ausable.

The Southern Division

Looking now to the southern half of today's Central Vermont, we first consider the New London, Willimantic & Springfield Railroad, chartered in 1847. Its Connecticut backers were flush with whaling money when they envisioned a connection with Massachusetts' Western Railroad at either Springfield or Palmer. A year later the company was aligned with the New London, Willimantic & Palmer Railroad, chartered in Massachusetts to meet the NLW&S. The two groups merged, using the latter corporate name. July 1848 saw ground-breaking just north of Norwich, and by May 1849 trains were running 30 miles between New London and Willimantic. All 66 miles to Palmer were operating by September 1850.

Unfortunately the costs of construction were much more than anticipated while revenues were far below projections. To increase revenue, the directors authorized an extension, completed in 1852, through downtown New London to connect with the New Haven & New London Railroad. They effected a track connection with the Norwich & Worcester in the fall of 1853, but several schemes for through New York-Boston passenger trains over a short stretch of its tracks came to nothing.

The company failed to meet bond interest payments in 1856 and went into receivership in January 1859. It was reorganized as the New London Northern, whose leaders assumed control April 1, 1861 with a more realistic debt—down from over $1.5 million to $600,000. Improvements were soon accomplished in both physical plant and equipment.

Again looking for expansion opportunity (specifically through business with the Vermont Central), in 1864 the NLN purchased the Amherst, Belchertown & Palmer Railroad—a line it had previously leased for seven months back in 1853—and by October 1866 completed another 15 miles north to Grout's Corner (later named Millers Falls) on the Vermont and Massachusetts Railroad (Fitchburg to Greenfield, Massachusetts). The V&M also owned a line 21 miles from Grout's Corner to Brattleboro—once its mainline but now a branch—and the V&M leased it to the Rutland (soon to be controlled by J. Gregory Smith) for ten years from 1870 to 1880. The New London Northern bought it in May 1880, completing its mainline, the eventual southern division of the Central Vermont. (Two small branches in Connecticut, at Fitchville and Montville, were subsequently added. The Ware River Railroad, completed to Gilbertville, Massa-chusetts, was briefly leased by the NLN between 1868 and 1873, after which it went to the Boston & Albany.)

A steamship line was added to the roster in June 1868, running between New London and New York City, a very important addition to its portfolio.

Smith interests leased the New London Northern in December 1871; a year and a half later the lease was assumed by the Central Vermont. It was still under lease 80 years later, when an actual purchase was finally made in December 1951.

A New Corporate Name

By 1873 the Vermont Central was at its largest—793 miles—controlling two mainlines between Bellows Falls and Burlington, separate southern routes to Chatham, New York and New London, Connecticut, separate northern routes to the Great Lakes at Ogdensburg, New York, and to St. Johns, Quebec, with a connection to Montreal. But the railroad was vastly overextended given the modest level of business, and this fatness was only exacerbated by the post-Civil War panic in 1873 (ironically caused largely by the overextended condition of America's railroads). The company reorganized that year as the Central Vermont, and the slimming down came quickly. The three small railroads in New York were almost immediately sold to the rising Delaware & Hudson. The Rutland's lease payments were negotiated down in 1875 (finally cancelled in 1896) and in 1877 both the Ogdensburg & Lake Champlain and the Harlem Extension leases were dropped (the latter, 115 miles from Rutland to Chatham, New York, had been held only since 1873).

Above: CV 2-8-0 No. 462 is passing the joint CV-Rutland depot (see page 15) at Alburgh on August 24, 1955. Steven R. Payne photo. **Below:** Just south of the East Alburgh trestle, the southbound Ambassador steams by on February 20, 1954. Included in the consist are a diner, an "American Flyer" coach, and a B&M stainless steel coach. John Gardner photo.

Central Vermont 63

Still, there were small expansions where management envisioned profits. A six-mile line from Montpelier to Barre was completed in July 1875 to exploit the lucrative granite trade. Business was so good that another eight miles were built to Williamstown in 1888.

Following the Recession of 1893 there were further reductions in size. By mid 1896 the CV had 512.4 miles owned, leased, or controlled. In 1898 the CV Rail*road* reorganized as CV Rail*way*, with the Grand Trunk owning two-thirds of the stock. In 1900 CV and B&M concluded a shared trackage agreement between Northfield, Massachusetts, and White River Junction.

Some very bold expansion was planned by Grand Trunk President Charles M. Hays. The Southern New England Railway was to be a CV-subsidiary linking the 55 miles between Palmer, Massachusetts, and Providence, Rhode Island; considerable construction was actually done. Hays also proposed exclusive CV track between Windsor and Brattleboro to free his road of B&M dependency. Then Smith perished with the *Titanic*, and both plans were dropped.

The CV came under control of the Canadian government in 1922 when the Canadian National Railways were assembled from several financially troubled railroads: Canadian Northern, Grand Trunk, Grand Trunk Pacific, Intercolonial, and National Transcontinental.

The flood of November 1927 virtually destroyed the CV between Essex Junction and White River Junction. Canadian National provided the funds for the 92-day repair job. Later in the year came receivership, lasting until 1929 when the road emerged as the Central Vermont Railway, Inc.

All across America the times were very hard on the railroads in the 1920s and 1930s, and it was during these years that the CV closed three marginal branches: the Brattleboro-South Londonderry branch (West River Railroad) in 1927; Essex Junction-Cambridge Junction (where it connected with the St. Johnsbury & Lake Champlain) in 1938; and the Barre-Williamstown branch in 1939.

World War II kept the railroad busy with troop movements and German war prisoners incarcerated in Canadian camps.

In 1946 a stevedores' strike in New York caused the closure of the New London-New York City ferry service, running since 1868.

Diesels arrived on the CV in 1941, two Alco-GE S2 switchers. Through freights were all powered by diesels beginning in 1953, and the last steam engine made its run in April 1957.

The 40-mile St. Armand Subdivision—East Swanton to St. Johns, Quebec—was abandoned in March 1955. Montpelier Junction-Barre was sold to Samuel Pinsly in 1958 (more in Chapter IV). Tracks between East Alburgh to Rouses Point, 8.3 miles, were abandoned in 1962, although access to the latter was available over CN via Cantic.

The Interstate Highway system gave a great boost to the trucking industry. Rail revenues suffered as freight loadings declined in the 1960s and 1970s, and with the withdrawal of U. S. mail contracts in 1965, quickly causing the cancellation of several local CV passenger trains.

The 1980s were checkered years for the CV. Encouraging developments included some new industry locating along the line, a judiciously improved physical plant, the rise of intermodal freight, strong trade in lumber and wood-chips, a computerized car control system, and ameliorated labor agreements allowing smaller crews and partial elimination of cabooses.

Losses in the early 1980s were troubling, caused by three major factors: 1) high inflation; 2) increased competition resulting from the deregulation of the railroads in 1980; and 3) the amalgamation of Maine Central, Boston & Maine, and Delaware & Hudson under Guilford Transportation Industries, which siphoned off vital traffic. CV's parent, Grand Trunk Corporation, was sufficiently concerned to put the road up for sale in December 1982, though no sale transpired.

The Central Vermont became owner of a part of Boston & Maine's Connecticut River line in August 1988. A dispute between Guilford Transportation Industries and Amtrak—who held that Guilford's virtual neglect of the track from Springfield to Windsor was limiting the *Montrealer* to 10 mph—resulted in Amtrak taking 49 miles of disputed trackage from Brattleboro to Windsor by eminent domain and selling it to a willing Central Vermont. The case went all the way to the Supreme Court, which ruled in Amtrak's favor on March 25 1992.

Net profits totaling over $3 million during 1985 and 1986 were subsequently matched with alarmingly growing losses into the 1990s. The CV was again placed on sale in late October 1993, and in all likelihood the railroad will see the turn of the century under a very different structure from that existing today. Yet this is a resilient time for America's railroads, which have shown great potential for survival and rebirth. The unfolding future of the CV will no doubt be an absorbing one.

Above: *Central Vermont Railway ticket, Iberville to St. Alexander, Quebec. Jack May collection.*

Right: *Canadian National 4-8-4 No. 6240, built by the Montreal Locomotive Works in the early 1940s, is laying it on heavily with a southbound freight at Swanton on September 14, 1951. The beautiful locomotive enjoyed scarcely 20 years of service. John Gardner photo.*

Above: C-Liner 9308 heads a freight at Swanton on July 5, 1959. Norton D. Clark collection. **Below:** Central Vermont Railway ticket, Stanbridge to St. Armand, Quebec. Jack May collection. **Bottom:** Gas-electric car 148 at Swanton in June 1953. David C. Bartlett photo.

Below: The hogger looks back on his fall foliage trip on October 2, 1954, at Swanton. The train's circle route from Montpelier included Montpelier Junction, St. Albans, Swanton, St. Johnsbury, Wells River, and Montpelier. John Gardner collection.

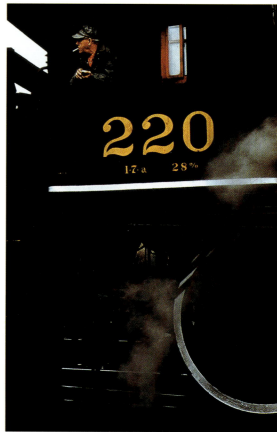

66   Green Mountain Rails

St. Albans was experiencing fine weather indeed on September 3, 1956. Russell F. Munroe made these two photographs, both showing the Ambassador at the venerable CV brick depot, built in 1867. Locomotive No. 5291 is a 4-6-2 built at Montreal in 1919 for the Canadian Government Railways. The office portion of the building stands today, though the trainshed, in bad repair, was torn down in September 1963.

Central Vermont

Four views of St. Albans and its environs.

Left: A double-headed freight pounds through the countryside behind CV 2-8-0 No. 466 and 2-10-4 No. 704 on April 18, 1952.

Below left: CV 4-8-2 No. 603 is on the turntable on August 1, 1953.

Bottom: A work train is grading roadbed for new track on August 1, 1953. Looks like the brass is on hand. Three photos by Stephen R. Payne.

Right: A hogger oils his charge in the fall of 1953. John Gardner photo.

Below: Central Vermont Railway ticket, Windsor to St. Albans, Jack May collection.

Central Vermont 69

Left: On October 12, 1956, Russell F. Munroe photographed the crew change on the Montrealer at St. Albans. Today's power is Canadian National Railways 4-8-4 No. 6173, built by Montreal Locomotive Works in April 1940.

Below left: On June 13 that year, the first section of the Montrealer has arrived at St. Albans just at first light behind Grand Trunk Western No. 6039, built by Baldwin in 1925, carrying green marker lights. A new head-end crew is waiting to board. The train is carrying a Pennsy baggage car and a B&M stainless combine. T. J. Donahue photo.

Above right: The Richford Branch was completed in December 1872 as the 28-mile Missisquoi Railroad to St. Albans. Central Vermont regularly used these two SW 1200s, Nos. 1510 and 1511, on the branch as power for the local freight. They are seen here on August 3, 1977 crossing the Missisquoi River heading south toward St. Albans. Ronald N. Johnson photo.

Below right: Six Central Vermont GPs are pulling train 447 northbound across the Georgia High Bridge on February 5, 1983. At left is an abutment from an earlier bridge structure. Al Irwin photo/John Gardner collection.

70   Green Mountain Rails

Both the Central Vermont and the Rutland passed through Colchester. The CV ran some ten miles east of the Rutland, and is pictured in the three photographs on this page.

Left: A blaze of summer wild flowers at Colchester encases the southbound Ambassador on July 4, 1954.

Center left: February 23, 1953 was one of those completely delightful sunny days in mid-winter which impart their own special beauty. Locomotive No. 603, a 4-8-2, is on the point, its steam obliterating the identity of its train.

Below left: Four years later, on February 3, 1957, the scene is a lot more dark and somber. This freight, also southbound, is pulled by 2-8-0 No. 465. Three photos by John Gardner.

72   Green Mountain Rails

CENTRAL VERMONT PASSENGER SERVICE

The Vermont Central went all out to please passengers. It carried Pullman Palace sleeping cars (the first to run was New York City to St. Albans) and Pullman drawing-room and parlor cars on all its expresses. Smoking cars graced the through trains. Complete meals were offered at scheduled stops at dining halls and restaurants. The road even installed Bible racks in each passenger car to appease the frowning clergy.

The Central Vermont actively promoted excursion service, with the 1876 Centennial in Philadelphia being an especially popular destination. That same year the *White Mountain Express* began running from Saratoga to the White Mountains (via CV from Burlington to Montpelier) during the summer months. It lasted until 1925.

The *Green Mountain Flyer*, usually associated with the Rutland, ran over CV rails north of Burlington from 1891 to 1900, when the Rutland built its causeway line to Rouses Point.

The famous *Montrealer-Washingtonian* was begun in 1924.

The New Haven Railroad originated a snow train called the *Ski Meister* in the late 1930s which departed New York on Fridays at 8:40 p.m., splitting into sections at White River Junction, three of which went over the CV. One travelled to Montpelier and Barre, one to Burlington, and one to St. Albans. These overnight trains featured Pullman sleepers, skiers' club cars, and ski service cars—baggage cars tarted up to sell ski equipment and offer service. Diners provided breakfast for 30¢ and 50¢, lunch for 90¢, and dinner for a dollar. Undoubtedly a lot of new friendships were forged on these trains.

In 1926 the CV replaced its Montreal-Boston *New England States Limited* with the *Ambassador*, an all-new train and the first to provide radio on board, for first class passengers. It was the CV's comfortable daily train from Montreal with sections for both New York and Boston splitting at White River Junction, typically carrying parlor car, diner, smoker, and coaches. The diner and parlor car were dropped in the early 1930s and replaced by a buffet club car. A new, faster schedule was announced in June 1938, featuring deluxe, air-conditioned coaches. In its last years, the *Ambassador* variously required a change of trains at White River Junction and Springfield on the New York run, and at White River Junction on the Boston leg, this last dropped completely by the B&M in January 1965. The CV continued to use the *Ambassador* name long after the B&M stopped using it in timetables in 1956.

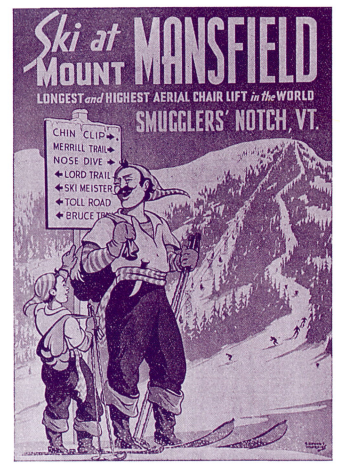

From the cover of the February 9, 1942 Central Vermont timetable. RWJ collection

On CV's southern division, beginning in 1924, one of two daily-except-Sunday, Brattleboro-New London round trips was covered by a Brill gas-electric car, replacing steam. Soon both runs had Brill cars. Subsequently the second run was cut, and for a time in the late 1930s the surviving run was replaced by a mixed-train, with the Brill car returning during the war.

The last two CV passenger trains, the *Ambassador*, and the *Montrealer-Washingtonian* (joint operation with Pennsylvania, New Haven, and Boston & Maine), were eliminated September 3, 1966. Amtrak restored the latter in late September 1972, calling both segments *Montrealer* beginning in 1973.

The route was changed in 1989 when Amtrak reinstated the *Montrealer* on an all-CV route via New London and Palmer, beginning July 18, 1989 after a 26-month hiatus. The new route, originally thought to be temporary, is still in operation. This was the first time since the war, when the Brill car operated, that CV's southern division hosted a passenger train.

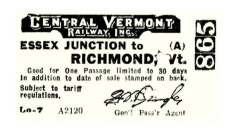

Central Vermont Railway ticket, Essex Junction to Richmond. Jack May collection.

74 Green Mountain Rails

Left: *CV 2-8-0 No. 463 is just pulling through the Essex Junction depot with a reefer train in March 1953. John Gardner photo.*

Below left: *Russell F. Munroe found CV 4-8-2 No. 602 taking water at the barn-like Essex Junction depot on July 12, 1953.*

Right: *On a starkly blue and white and very cold February 16, 1952, a CV freight has just passed through Essex Junction. The depot is just visible in the distance. John Gardner photo.*

Bottom: *The southbound Ambassador is loading express and passengers at Essex Junction on February 11, 1961. On the point is GP-9 4925. The car following the RPO is from the Grand Trunk Western. Charles G. Parsons photo/William P. Nixon collection.*

Central Vermont

Left: *Lumber products have remained a staple of Vermont railroads since their creation. A wood-chip train is westbound at Winooski, between the mainline at Essex Junction and Burlington on August 9, 1985, behind RS-11s 3606 and 3612. Russell F. Munroe photo.*

Below: *The Rocket is northbound at Jonesville with a piggy-back train on September 9, 1980 behind RS-11 3609, the second CV RS-11 to carry this number. The first was wrecked in 1979. This one is the former Norfolk & Western No. 367. Ronald N. Johnson photo.*

76   Green Mountain Rails

Above: The Ambassador is at Waterbury in October 1954 behind Canadian National 4-8-4 No. 6218. At left is RS-3 1859, only in its second month of service. **Below:** Grand Trunk Western 4-8-2 No. 6039 waits east of Waterbury for an 8-car northbound Ambassador behind RS-3 1860 to clear the mainline. The 1859 and 1860 were the only two RS-3s to be painted in CV colors; they ran on the CV from 1954 to 1958, when they went to the CN. Just two other RS-3s served the CV—two Grant Trunk freight units between 1954 and 1957. Two photos by T. J. Donahue.

Above: *At Montpelier Junction very early on the morning of July 30, 1966, the* Montrealer *pauses for head-end business and passenger loading. The long consist requires two diesels, GP-9s 4927 and 4929, both built by EMD in 1957. George F. Melvin photo/J. Emmons Lancaster collection.*

Below: *Train 444 is southbound near West Braintree behind five Central Vermont GP-9s and a Canadian National H-420 on September 29, 1985. Ronald N. Johnson photo.*

78   Green Mountain Rails

Above: *A CV freight is passing the attractive brick Randolph depot on May 10, 1958. Note the baggage car ahead of the caboose. Stanley W. Cook photo.* **Below:** *Just outside Randolph, David C. Bartlett made this dramatic photo of the mighty 2-10-4 No. 707 highballing the northbound* Vermonter *at the crack of dawn in August 1953 with five head-end cars and two Pullmans. The Pullmans were carried on the* Montrealer *between New York and White River Junction, where they were switched onto the* Vermonter, *making local stops to the end of the run at St. Albans.*

Central Vermont   79

Above: Central Vermont train 447 is switching cars at Bethel before heading north in January 1986. Today's power is four CV GP-9s and two from the Grand Trunk. Ronald N. Johnson photo. **Above right:** It's Thursday, August 12, 1965, and the northbound Ambassador has arrived at Bethel at 4:49 p.m. behind GP-9 4923. Its new paint scheme is a nice match for the New Haven coaches which were often used on this train. **Center right:** Shown here on October 12, 1962, the depot at South Royalston had an unusually grand center window. Two photos by Stanley W. Cook. **Below right:** The Ambassador is northbound at Bethel in July 1959. Central Vermont's green, black, and dulux gold paint scheme was especially elegant and distinguished. Modelers take note of the black bands on the top and bottom of the above-the-sash green panel. Arthur E. Mitchell photo.

80   Green Mountain Rails

Central Vermont 81

82　Green Mountain Rails

Above left: In a striking Vermont setting, a northbound freight is near Sharon behind Grand Trunk diesel power, Nos. 4446, 4905, 4927, and 4449, on May 30, 1971. John F. Kane photo.

Above: The sun is setting this January 30, 1951 and the long shadows are falling across CV 4-8-2 No. 603 and the coaling tower in the White River Junction yard. Stephen R. Payne photo.

Left: In December 1956, Central Vermont 2-10-4 No. 707 passes this dazzling blue and white snow scene at West Hartford. David C. Bartlett photo.

Right: May 10, 1950 finds an avid gathering of rail enthusiasts at White River Junction. Presently they are admiring the 603, soon to depart for Montreal. Perhaps they arrived on the Ambassador's "American Flyer" coach in the background. Note the ball signal as well as the famous locomotive weather vane on top of the depot. Norton D. Clark collection.

Central Vermont 83

Above: The southbound *Ambassador* is soon to arrive at White River Junction on September 3, 1952 in this dramatic shot by Allan W. Styffe. *Below:* A railfan excursion has brought admiring photographers to White River Junction on June 14, 1953. CV 2-8-0 No. 474 and 2-10-4 No. 704 have caught their immediate attention. The locos were built by Alco in 1923 and 1928, respectively. Russell F. Munroe photo. **Left:** Central Vermont Railway Ticket, Roxbury to White River Junction. Jack May collection.

Above: The elegant lines of CV's No. 704 are immediately evident in this broadside photo made on June 14, 1953. Ten of these locos were built for the CV at Alco's Schenectady Works in 1928. Those aluminum window bands on the B&M "American Flyer" cars were certainly classy. Russell F. Munroe photo. **Below:** Four decades later, on June 20, 1982, a northbound freight departs White River Junction behind five GP-9s: B&M 1711 and 1826; and CV 4558, 4549, and 4550. John Ross Photo/J. Emmons Lancaster collection.

Central Vermont

Above** and **Left: *Arthur E. Mitchell chased a southbound freight after it crossed the Connecticut River at Windsor into New Hampshire onto B&M rails, on February 19, 1955. The late-afternnon landscape is striking in the extreme.*

Below: *Central Vermont Railway ticket, Windsor to Northfield. Jack May collection.*

86   Green Mountain Rails

Above: *It's a grim December 28, 1954 as CV 2-10-4 No. 707 heads south with a freight through Claremont Junction, New Hampshire. The presence of people on the platform indicates a passenger train is due. Amtrak still stops here, though the building is now a restaurant. Norton D. Clark collection.*
Below: *2-10-4 No. 708 is bringing a northbound freight into Bellows Falls on a more pleasant day in the summer of 1954. Arthur E. Mitchell photo.*

For the three decades that they travelled on the Central Vermont, the road's ten 2-10-4s were the largest steam power in New England. Stephen R. Payne photographed these two locomotives three days apart at Westminster in January 1951. No. 703, **above***, was shot on the 12th while No. 708,* **below***, was shot on the 9th.*

Above: *The Connecticut River at Brattleboro is a wonderful setting to photograph trains, especially the magical forces of steam power. CV 2-8-0 No. 473 is on the fill on April 7, 1952, while **below,** 2-8-0 No. 460 is shown on a much colder January 9, 1951. Two photos by Stephen R. Payne.*

Above: At the Brattleboro passenger station the local switcher has completed its task of re-railing the gondola behind it, which had one truck completely on the ground. The crew takes a brief respite in the shade while waiting for a southbound train to clear on a hot summer afternoon in 1954. Arthur E. Mitchell photo. *Below:* Some two years earlier, on April 17, 1952, two CV 2-8-0s, Nos. 451 and 462, await assignments at the Brattleboro engine house. Both are products of Schenectady: 1916 and 1923, respectively. Stephen R. Payne photo.
Right: Central Vermont Railway ticket, Brattleboro to Three Rivers. Jack May collection.

90 Green Mountain Rails

The passing up of orders was a sacred railroad ritual, intended to ensure the safe and efficient operation of trains. Before the telegraph and signals, train orders were the only method of control. A southbound CV freight at East Northfield, Massachusetts, here receives orders from the shared B&M-CV agent. Note that as he hands up the orders to the fireman, **above**, with his right hand, he holds the other set in his left, which he holds for the conductor, **below**, in the caboose as it brings up the rear. Two photos from the Leon Onofri collection.

Central Vermont

Above: While head-end business is being attended to, our engine crew is making a check of the running gear on No. 603 at East Northfield. Just into Massachusetts, East Northfield was the junction of the Central Vermont and the Boston & Maine. From here north to Brattleboro where they met again, the B&M ran in New Hampshire while the CV ran in Vermont. Moving south, the two roads moved further and further apart. The B&M terminated in Springfield, the CV at New London. *Below:* At Millers Falls, Massachusetts, the CV crossed the Fitchburg Division of the B&M. The station was a shared operation. Here are three freight trains passing through at once. At left is a westbound B&M freight, while at right there are two CV freights having a meet. The depot was badly damaged by a B&M freight derailment in February 1963. Two photos from the Leon Onofri collection.

Above right: Here we can see just how very active Millers Falls was. Two CV freights are meeting, and two other CV locos, helpers probably, are in the background. Note the two distinctly different styles of order boards on the depot for the CV and the B&M. At one time the agent lived upstairs in the apartment.

Right: On a brown and gold October 20, 1955, 2-8-0 No. 465 leads its train across the Connecticut River at Millers Falls. Two photos by Stephen R. Payne.

92   Green Mountain Rails

94 Green Mountain Rails

Left: *A remarkable show of double-headed steam exhaust at Millers Falls on April 7, 1952, with CV 2-8-0s Nos. 462 and 473. Note the tell-tale, a long-forgotten implement of railroading. Stephen R. Payne photo.*

Below left: *CV 2-8-0 No. 467 is backing onto train 430, the Newsboy, serving as a helper to get the train over some hilly country to the south. Today's Newsboy power is a pair of Canadian National C-Liners. Northbound train 491 waits at right behind a CN diesel. T. J. Donahue photo.*

Right: *Blasting through a curve amidst snow and pine trees is CV 2-8-0 No. 451 at Montague, Massachusetts, on December 28, 1950.*

Bottom: *Still at Montague, but on a considerably warmer April 7, 1952, 2-8-0s Nos. 462 and 473 are dragging their freight above the highway. Two photos by Stephen R. Payne.*

Below: *Central Vermont Railway ticket, Palmer to Three Rivers. Jack May collection.*

Central Vermont

Above: CV 2-8-0 451 has a way freight southbound at Amherst, Massachusetts. T. J. Donahue photo.

Left: Norton D. Clark found two freights meeting on May 27, 1962 at Amherst. GP-9 4556 is in the lead. Three years later it went to the Grand Trunk Western.

Above right: A handsome pair of C-Liners flys across a high fill in a rural setting in Amherst, with white flags flying on April 12, 1955. No. 8714 is in the lead. Alan W. Styffe photo.

Right: CV's manifest freight, the Newsboy, passes the southbound way freight at North Amherst. Newsboy power is C-Liner 9338, while CV 2-8-0 No. 470 is on the way freight. T. J. Donahue photo.

Central Vermont 97

Above: Here's another glimpse of the 451 at Amherst, this time on a blue and white December 28, 1950. The red brick depot with its green trim is still looking pretty good. *Below:* The 470 has just three cars and a caboose on October 22, 1955 as it passes through Belchertown's autumn foliage.

We're on the big curve at Palmer, Massachusetts, on December 6, 1950, as a long freight is moving some heavy tonnage. Putting out a handsome white cloud are CV 2-8-0s Nos. 471 and 468, while on the rear end are two cabooses, Nos. 4011 and 4007. Four photos by Stephen R. Payne.

100 Green Mountain Rails

Above left and Left: Norton D. Clark recorded the 451 doing its work in Palmer, Massachusetts, on April 19, 1956. It's late in the day and the crew is about to put up for the night as they head onto the Armstrong turntable.

Above: On November 14, 1949 this CV freight at Palmer is running behind 2-8-0s Nos. 464 and 462, separated by three boxcars to keep from exceeding bridge weight loads on this section of the line.
Stephen R. Payne photo.

Right: The Newsboy blasts over Monson Hill behind 2-8-0 No. 464. T. J. Donahue photo.

Below: Central Vermont Railway ticket, Palmer to Belchertown. Jack May collection.

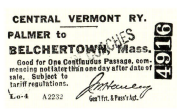

Central Vermont 101

Above: In a sight common on the Central Vermont, a steam helper assists a diesel-powered freight in hilly terrain. A 2-8-0 is ahead of the two C-Liners. The train is dramatically beautiful in the gold light of a winter late afternoon, its smoke looking like thick gray cotton as it approaches Monson Hill.
T. J. Donahue photo.

Right: With white flags flying, 2-8-0s 474 and 467 are pulling hard at Monson on August 15, 1952.

Far Right: And here's another fine portrait of a 2-8-0 at Monson. No. 462 is pulling up the hill on December 6, 1950. Two photos by Stephen R. Payne.

At State Line crossing between Massachusetts and Connecticut here is a contrast in the seasons. **Above:** A southbound way freight is behind 2-8-0 No. 450 on a cold, clear day. T. J. Donahue photo. **Below:** The earth is greening on May 14, 1955 as another way freight works its way south behind 2-8-0 No. 472. Norton D. Clark photo.

T. J. Donahue photographed this meet of northbound train 491 with the southbound way freight behind 2-8-0 No. 450 at Stafford Springs, Connecticut. **Above:** A demonstrative crew member gives the photographer an emphatic "thumb-up" sign as the freight heads through. The way freight's brakeman is walking to the switch. **Below:** With the northbound freight now gone by, the way freight reclaims the mainline.

Central Vermont 105

Above: *On an idyllic summer day in 1952, Connecticut Public Utility Inspectors have left their autos at Mansfield station and boarded a special train of CV business cars for their annual run over the CV. A freight waits in the hole for the special to proceed. Arthur E. Mitchell photo.* ***Below:*** *A few months later CV 2-8-0 No. 484 is at the same location for switching chores. Allan W. Styffe photo.*

106   Green Mountain Rails

Above: Alan W. Styffe waited on a cold and windy March 22, 1956 for the southbound way freight at South Coventry, Connecticut. Today's power is 2-8-0 No. 450. The depot is showing signs of neglect, evidenced by the broken windows and the long-unpainted CV herald. **Below:** It's early morning in June 1956 and the low sun accentuates the lines and shapes of a northbound way freight enroute to Willimantic. T. J. Donahue photo.

Willimantic, Connecticut, was a fascinating railroad town, the crossroads of three separate rail routes: the New Haven's Midland Division, its Providence to Hartford line, and the Central Vermont mainline. **Above:** The southbound local from Palmer is in front of the Willimantic passenger station in 1954 in an informative view of the yard and its surroundings. Arthur E. Mitchell photo. **Below:** Bridge Street crossing had a full-time tender—then a commonplace on American railroads. Take special note of him and his stop sign, his order hoop, his shanty at the left, and especially the cast iron "Rail Road Crossing" sign. He also operated the unusual CV signal on page 110, located just a few steps out of sight to the left of the shanty. This trackage through Willimantic was New Haven iron, and the Bridge Street operator was a New Haven employee. The local freight with 2-8-0 No. 452 on the point was photographed on October 13, 1954. by T. J. Donahue.

Above: C-Liner 8706 is getting a helping hand from 2-8-0 No. 467 on March 19, 1955, a frequent occurrence in this hilly countryside. Allan W. Styffe photo. **Below:** Manifest freight 491 departs Willimantic behind Canadian National GP-9s 4524 and 4534—how clean the diesels were kept—with helper 2-8-0 No. 467 cut in eight cars back. T. J. Donahue photo.

Left: This gallows-like signal was unique to the CV's Willimantic operation and is well known among followers of the railroad. *Above:* No. 464 has cut off from its train, and has pulled up to the water plug where it appears to have overflowed its tank. Two photos by T. J. Donahue. *Below:* The double-heading of freights on the CV in Massachusetts and Connecticut was very frequent because the tonnage was heavy and the hills were numerous. Here two freights pass near Bridge Street. The northbound, train 491, is 12 hours late, while the southbound, train 490, is on time. Arthur E. Mitchell photo from 1954. *Right and Below right:* T. J. Donahue made these two photographs of way freights in close proximity. The first is of 2-8-0 No. 464 near Montville, Connecticut, while the second is of a way freight in the town proper. Both trains are northbound.

Central Vermont 111

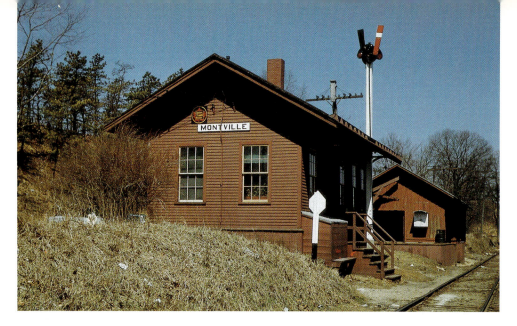

Above left: The Montville station is in lovely condition, well kept-up, with a plant in the window. T. J. Donahue photo.

Center left: CV 2-8-0 No. 452 has caboose 4007 for some switching at Fitchville, Connecticut, on March 22, 1956. Alan W. Styffe photo.

New London, Connecticut, an historic seaport, was the southern terminus of the Central Vermont. It interchanged freight here with the New Haven Railroad, and up through the mid-1940s even ran daily passenger trains here from Brattleboro.

Below left: Several Central Vermont and Grand Trunk GP-9s—including CV 4927 and 4549—grace the New London engine terminal on May 11, 1970, along with Canadian National caboose 79089. Alan W. Styffe photo.

Above right: CV 2-8-0s Nos. 470 and 476 are at the engine terminal for servicing and turning on December 7, 1952. In the left background are the giant piers for the highway bridge over the Thames River.

Below right: It's 7:00 p.m. and there's not much light remaining. Still, Arthur E. Mitchell carefully recorded this double-headed freight departing the New London yard on Kodachrome with an ASA speed of 10.

By May 13, 1979 spring has bloomed rich and full through the Green Mountain state. Here at Duxbury, Jim Shaughnessy created this majestic portrait of a southbound Central Vermont freight crossing the Winooski River behind six brightly painted diesel locomotives. The first three are CV GP-9s: 4550, 4548, and 4923. Next come two RS-11s: Duluth, Winnipeg & Pacific 3605, and CV 3611, and finally CV GP-9 4926 brings up the rear of the power.

Canadian National's American lines had considerable freedom, evidenced by their varied paint schemes, and some swapping of motive power resulted in this cornucopia on the CV. The green with yellow bands of the lead unit was an employee suggestion, and eventually became the standard on CV. The blue and red design originated on the Grand Trunk Western, while the black and red combination came from CN. Finally, the red-orange from the DW&P provided just the right splash of brilliance.

Interestingly, the small trees in the right foreground were cut down as part of regular maintenance by the railroad, and were not the work of the photographer, as some assumed when this photo first appeared in the November 1979 Trains magazine.

Central Vermont

Top: Combine No. 113 was an especially interesting piece of vintage StJ&LC equipment. It accommodated passengers, baggage, and U. S. Mail on a Monday thru Saturday mixed train to Swanton. Maine Central E-7 709 has come to St. Johnsbury from Portland with the daily train and will soon return. **Above:** No. 27 was an 0-6-0 built by Baldwin in 1923, purchased by StJ&LC in 1949 from the McKeesport Connecting Railroad in Pennsylvania, then sold in 1955 to the Rock of Ages Corporation, where it was scrapped in 1959. Two photos by Arthur E. Mitchell.

III

ST. JOHNSBURY & LAKE CHAMPLAIN

St. Johnsbury & Lamoille County • Lamoille Valley Railroad

Erastus Fairbanks of St. Johnsbury, Vermont, scale manufacturer, was also president and chief stockholder of the St. Johnsbury & Lake Champlain Railroad and a strict observer of the Sabbath. No trains were scheduled for Sunday operation, and his orders were that not a wheel should turn on that day. The operating officials, however, sometimes found it necessary to do some shifting of cars on Sunday, occasionally to run a work-train or in winter to send out a snow-plow to keep the line open. It behooved them to do this very early in the morning or as quietly as could be, so that Mr. Fairbanks in his mansion would not hear the noise. Accordingly, engineers were warned to "hook her up" as near noiselessly as possible, not to use the bell, blow off steam or use the whistle, though there were some crossings where these warning sounds were legally required. As the railroad leaves town westward up a stiff grade, noiseless operation took some doing, but they often got away with it. They well knew that if Mr. Fairbanks heard so much as a whisper from an engine on Sunday, he would go down to the office on Monday morning and severely reprimand all parties concerned, with a threat of discharge if it happened again.

John S. Kendall
A Treasury of Railroad Folklore

The St. Johnsbury & Lake Champlain Railroad—operating today as the Lamoille Valley Railroad—never completely fulfilled its original purpose: a bridge route to the Great Lakes from Portland, Maine. Its few, intermittent years of black ink were anomalies among long periods of thin revenue and high expenses.

The railroad fever sweeping the U. S. in the mid-19th century touched St. Johnsbury, Vermont in a tangible way in 1850 with the arrival of the Connecticut & Passumpsic Rivers Railroad, building on its way north to Canada. Locals perceived the vast potential of an east-west route between the lakes and the sea, but they lacked sufficient resources to effect construction. It wasn't until the city of Portland, Maine, voted funds in 1868 that progress was achieved. The ensuing venture comprised three contiguous railroads in Vermont: Essex County Railroad, Montpelier & St. Johnsbury Railroad, and Lamoille Valley Railroad. Together they formed the independent Portland & Ogdensburg Railroad—Vermont Division.

Trackage between Portland and Swanton was eventually completed in July 1877, but the toll of construction was so great and the financial base so poor that receivership followed quickly in October.

With the debts settled one year later, the St. Johnsbury & Lake Champlain was created from the three roads of the Vermont Division. Another 12 miles of track built as the Lamoille Valley Extension Railroad took the line from Swanton to Rouses Point, New York. Almost immediately, success was stifled by the Central Vermont—new owner of the Ogdensburg & Lake Champlain—with its refusal to interchange cars with the StJ&LC, thus thwarting the young road's outlet to the lakes. With no seeming hope of use, the new, 12-mile extension was ripped up scarcely six months after laying.

Frustrated stockholders sold the railroad, which shortly came under the control of the Boston & Lowell, an ambitious road which envisioned its own, independent route to Montreal via part of the StJ&LC. This plan, too, was dropped when the B&L leased the Connecticut & Passumpsic Rivers railroad instead. Soon after, the B&L

Three GE 70-ton locomotives were commonly run together, yielding the necessary horsepower for the steep grades without overloading the aging bridges on the line. This bucolic scene, with Nos. 48, 54, and 46, was captured on film in May 1966 by J. Emmons Lancaster.

was absorbed into the Boston & Maine.

To protect its stock investment, the B&M leased the StJ&LC in 1895. In 1902 the former Essex County Railroad (trackage east from St. Johnsbury to Lunenburg on the Connecticut River) was leased to the Maine Central, giving it direct access to St. Johnsbury.

By 1925 the Boston & Maine realized that it had acquired too many marginal lines. The road's General Manager (later President) Edward S. French—who advocated local management as the only way to solvency—became President of the StJ&LC (a year later the Montpelier & Wells River would be similarly reorganized). The new management was sorely tested in November 1927 when major flooding caused 160 washouts costing nearly half a million dollars in repairs.

During the next several years the freight business improved slowly while passenger revenues continued to decline. When bonds fell due in 1944—the B&M being owed $3 million—the StJ&LC filed for bankruptcy. Yet income was on the rise, so on January 24, 1948, after lengthy discussion, the road was reorganized and incorporated as the St. Johnsbury & Lamoille County, and operations continued. The old B&M K-7s were retired with the acquisition of 70-ton General Electric diesels.

The B&M finally sold out completely to local interests in the early 1950s. The mixed train was cancelled in 1956, and the U. S. Mail contract along with it. The milk business was disappearing fast, too. A new owner was need-

The decline of business continued. New England's industrial base was fast disappearing, and the railroad, down to a 10 mph maximum, was scarcely able to accommodate through traffic. In the fall of 1972 the segment between Morrisville and St. Johnsbury was embargoed; Pinsly filed for abandonment, citing absence of profit potential. He said that trucks could handle better what little work there was.

The state stepped in, via its newly created Vermont Transportation Authority, and arranged for Pinsly to withdraw. A local management group under Bruno Loati was eventually selected to operate the line, now called Lamoille County Railroad, with Vermont remaining as owner. In April 1974 the name reverted to St. Johnsbury & Lamoille County.

Further business set-backs again caused failure, and the company went out of business in 1976. During a short tenure under Morrison-Knudsen Corporation, the name became Vermont Northern. But Morrison-Knudsen departed when the expected and profitable work for track rehabilitation was awarded to a rival, after a disagreement with the state.

In 1978 the railroad, now locally operated by its major shippers, became the Lamoille Valley Railroad, with the state contributing $16 million in operating funds and a track rehabilitation program. In 1980 agreement was made with the CV to interchange traffic at St. Albans instead of Fonda Junction., eliminating some trackage, with the CV agreeing to service StJ&LC customers in the Swanton area.

Passenger service on the railroad was never very profitable, and by 1938 trains ran only as far west as Cambridge Junction., where passengers could connect with the CV for Burlington. Regular passenger service ended in 1944, while the mixed train lasted until 1956. The passenger excursions which have become so popular started in 1985, adding some much needed revenue.

The Lamoille Valley Railroad purchased 27 miles of Maine Central's former Mountain Division in 1984 (St. Johnsbury to Whitefield, New Hampshire) from Guilford Transportation Industries, calling it the Twin State Railroad. This new source of revenue kept the road going after there was no more freight west of St. Johnsbury. In 1989 both the LVRC and Twin State were bought by CSF Acquisitions. The new owners kept the Lamoille Valley name for the original route, while trackage east of St. Johnsbury became the New Hampshire & Vermont Railroad, now extending over former B&M branches to Berlin and Groveton, New Hampshire.

About this tenacious and scenic up-country line, former Lamoille Valley and Twin State General Manager Edward A. Lewis said it best: "The real miracle is that so many folks have worked together for so many years to keep this very marginal line in place in the face of natural disasters and financial failures. It is a real story of community success and perseverances."

ed who could fund improvements, and a long-aborning sale to the H. E. Salzberg Co. was finally consummated in 1959. In his six-year tenure, Salzberg was plagued by a variety of ills—the most threatening being the inadequate state of the physical plant to handle larger and more frequent through-freight loads—and he applied for abandonment in 1965. Neither the Maine Central nor the Central Vermont was interested in the property. Samuel Pinsly—Salzberg's brother in law—bought it in 1967. Significant improvements were made, including the purchase of reconditioned GP-9s and RS-3s, and the now famous Fisher Bridge was saved by the addition of steel supports placed underneath. It remains the last covered bridge on an operating railroad in New England.

St. Johnsbury & Lake Champlain

(Eastern Standard Time)

MI	TABLE 1 WEST BOUND TRAINS Stations	51 Pass. Ex Sun.	75 Mixed Ex. Sun.	77 Mixed Sun.
		am	pm	am
0 0	Lv St. Johnsbury, Vt., St.J.&L.C.R.R.	4 00	2 00	4 30
11 5	Danville	4 55	3 12	f 5 15
14 9	West Danville	f 5 05	3 24	f 5 25
23 9	Walden	5 15	3 37	f 5 35
27 8	Greensboro	5 42	3 69	f 5 58
31 0	East Hardwick	5 55	4 09	f 6 13
34 7	Hardwick	6 15	4 21	f 6 30
41 0	Wolcott	6 30		
48 9	Morrisville	6 50	5 00	f 7 10
51 6	Hyde Park	7 10	5 15	f 7 18
56 4	Johnson	7 25	5 30	f 7 28
64 3	Ar Cambridge Jct.	7 45	5 50	f 7 45
64 3	Lv Cambridge Jct., St.J.&L.C.R.R.		5 50	
74 2	East Fairfield		f 6 25	f 8 07
78 4	Fairfield		f 6 50	f 8 22
83 1	Sheldon			
84 6	Sheldon Jct.		f 7 16	f 8 40
87 4	East Highgate		f 7 25	f 8 48
90 9	Highgate			
96 1	Ar Swanton		7 55	9 15
		am	pm	am

MI	TABLE 2 EAST BOUND TRAINS Stations	52 Mixed Ex. Sun.	74 Ex. Sun.	76 Mixed Sun. Only
		am	am	am
0 0	Lv Swanton, Vt., St.J.&L.C.R.R.		9 15	9 45
5 2	Highgate			
8 6	East Highgate		f 9 43	f10 12
11 5	Sheldon Jct.		f 10 00	f10 22
13 0	Sheldon			
17 7	Fairfield		f10 25	f10 45
21 9	East Fairfield		f10 37	f10 55
31 8	Ar Cambridge Jct.		11 00	f11 25
31 8	Lv Cambridge Jct., St.J.&L.C.R.R.	8 15	11 10	
39 7	Johnson	8 35	11 29	f11 42
44 5	Hyde Park	8 47		f11 52
47 2	Morrisville	9 08	12 05	12 15
55 1	Wolcott	9 26		
61 4	Hardwick	9 43	12 40	12 51
65 1	East Hardwick	10 00	12 55	1 09
68 3	Greensboro	10 12	1 05	1 20
76 4	Walden	10 50	f 2 00	f 2 02
81 2	West Danville	f11 05	f 2 14	f 2 13
84 6	Danville	11 17	2 25	2 25
96 1	Ar St. Johnsbury, Vt.	11 50	3 00	3 00
		am	pm	pm

f Stops on signal

Far left: Delivered in 1948, No. 46 was the first of 11 GE 70-ton StJ&LC diesels. The road was contracted to perform switching for CP and MEC at St. Johnsbury. Here it works the Alouette in July 1954. Arthur E. Mitchell photo.

Left: This is the complete public timetable of the St. Johnsbury & Lamoille County Railroad from April 29, 1951. Conway Scenic Railway collection.

Below left: An eastbound Lamoille Valley Railroad passenger train is east of Wolcott on May 30, 1990. Jim Shaughnessy photo.

Right: This wreck at Hardwick on June 13, 1963 is typical of the many plaguing the line then. Dave Engman photo.

Below: GP-7s 201 and 200 emerge from the Fisher Bridge with a freight on June 22, 1971. J. Emmons Lancaster photo.

St. Johnsbury & Lake Champlain 121

Left and Below left: *Richard Sanborn chased this westbound freight through the snowy countryside on December 5, 1970, shown here at the Danville station, and coming up out of St. Johnsbury, respectively. The two StJ&LC GP-7s, Nos. 200 and 201, were purchased from the New York Central in October 1967.*

Right: *At St. Johnsbury the two GPs are followed by Alco RS-3 203, an ex-Great Northern diesel purchased in 1968. Russell F. Munroe made this photo on a dank April day in 1970. The road bought five RS-3s in total.*

Bottom: *A Lamoille Valley Alco RS-3m is eastbound over the Connecticut River, between Vermont and New Hampshire, on the Twin State Railroad in September 1984. Ron Johnson photo.*

Below: *St. Johnsbury & Lamoille County ticket, Jack May collection.*

St. Johnsbury & Lake Champlain   123

Top: *Rock of Ages 0-6-0 No. 6 is switching at Graniteville in 1956. The photo is from the collection of Dwight A. Smith, and was taken by his mother, Beatrice.* **Above:** *Montpelier & Barre No. 21 is exploring the quarry at Barre on August 28, 1969, with a railfan excursion. Russell F. Munroe photo.*

IV

IN GRANITE COUNTRY
Montpelier & Wells River • Barre & Chelsea • Montpelier & Barre

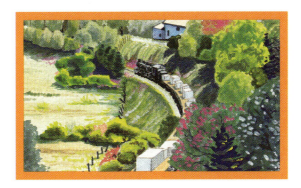

A deep-throated whistle announced the arrival of the train as it labored up an incline past the giant, spruce-flanked sign which read: WELCOME TO GRANITETOWN, VERMONT, THE LARGEST GRANITE CENTER IN THE WORLD. Most of the twenty passengers in the Granitetown coach were men. They peered intently from the windows at the greening countryside which rolled gently upward to the darker sky line of the Green Mountains, and which was thinly spangled now by the April sunshine of late afternoon.

Mari Tomasi
Like Lesser Gods

Two contrasting themes colored the intense desire for rail service in Montpelier, Vermont in the 1850s. First was a growing need to move goods more rapidly and less expensively in these increasingly productive times. Second was the lingering anger over former Governor Paine having maneuvered his Vermont Central to bypass Montpelier proper, deigning only to proffer service by way of a 1.5 mile branch from the mainline. With the VC—completed from Windsor to Burlington in 1849—having treated them in so cavalier a fashion on the west, Montpelierites looked hopefully to the east. After all, these were the days when there were myriad schemes to link the ports of Boston and Portland with Great Lakes shipping; the VC was not the only game in town.

With the difficult financial conditions of the late 1850s and the devastating effects of the Civil War behind them—and encouraged by the dual presence of the Connecticut & Passumpsic Rivers Railroad at Wells River and, just across the river, with the Boston, Concord & Montreal at Woodsville, New Hampshire—local leaders incorporated the Montpelier & Wells River Railroad in November 1867. Regular service began six years later in November 1873. It was a scenic railroad, managing to include nine covered bridges in its 38 miles of curvaceous trackage on grades reaching 2%.

As with neighboring railroads in the farm country, the dairy industry brought a lot of business. Butter shipments to Boston began in July 1874, with a special refrigerated car leaving every Monday morning for the hub. It was an exciting time. The M&WR line's presence facilitated the *White Mountain Express* in 1876 via Saratoga, Burlington, and Montpelier to New Hampshire's mountain resorts—completely up to date with Westinghouse air brakes. A through parlor car from Ogdensburg, New York, to Old Orchard Beach, Maine, was another colorful feature. Telegraph operation was incorporated into the M&WR in 1876.

The road was undercapitalized—sadly so common then—and it was in receivership already by 1876. After some troublesome litigation it was reorganized by its original officers in 1877. The road made a profit in 1878, thanks to the fast-growing lumber trade, ice cutting in winter, and a seemingly endless demand for paving stones.

Barre, Vermont, had long since become famous for its prolific granite quarries, and both the M&WR and the Central Vermont built branches here, six miles southeast of the state capitol. The CV came first, in 1875, while the M&WR was 14 years behind, although it held the advantage with a much better engineered right-of-way. The business was very lucrative right from the start; there were even occasional shortages of freight cars—one in 1917 was particularly acute. Quite naturally, the CV vigorously opposed this rival branch to Barre. Originally

In Granite Country 125

Barre & Chelsea train No. 4 is just arriving at Wells River late in the afternoon this beautiful July 15, 1950. Its daily-except-Sunday trip from Montpelier covered 40 miles in just over two and a half hours. Of the nine interim stops, five were "flags." Preston Johnson photo.

called the Barre Branch Railroad, it was leased to the M&WR in 1893 and 1894 and merged in 1913. The line was double-tracked between Montpelier and Barre in 1891 to accommodate the many trains. Even though first in Barre, the CV never pressed its advantage to build into the quarries; granite was still being hauled into town by horses. The M&WR financed the Barre Railroad to do just this, completing it in 1889, thus trumping the CV. At the same time, it built the Barre Branch Railroad from its own mainline into Barre, connecting with the Barre Railroad after only three month's opposition in the courts by the CV. This profitable little railroad, with its midway switchback, 5% grades, and roster of saddlebacks, was affectionately known as the "Sky Route to the Quarries."

Today it's useful to recognize just how important rail passenger service was to Americans in earlier times, especially in the countryside. There were two daily round-trips on the M&WR when it opened in 1873: one mail- and one mixed-train. An express was added in 1875, a stock train in 1878, and a poultry train in 1879. In 1881 there were three round trips, the service level for many years. When the Barre Branch Railroad opened in 1889, there were three daily round trips; a popular commuter service was begun in 1881. Eventually there would be nine round trips at the peak in 1898, soon reduced to six when a competing trolley line opened. By 1889 there was a daily through coach from Barre to Boston. The same year saw the first Sunday excursion (deeply frowned upon by local moral leaders), and summer excursions soon became popular and very common. Service beginning in 1883 from Montreal via Montpelier to Wells River and points south surely helped the locals feel they were every bit as good as the CV. Civic pride swelled notably when President Benjamin Harrison visited the M&WR in August 1891 while touring Vermont by rail. The peak year for passenger service was 1910, with 134,000 riders. A Burlington-Bretton Woods parlor car was featured in 1913. Perhaps the last gasp of luxury came in the winter of 1927-28 when a Barre-Montpelier-Boston overnight Pullman was carded.

The marked success of the M&WR was duly noticed by Charles Mellon, President of the New Haven Railroad and its new ward, the Boston & Maine. The B&M had grown mightily toward the end of the century, including absorption of the Connecticut River Railroad in 1893 for access into the heart of New Hampshire and Vermont. It was ripe for the picking when the New Haven moved in during 1907. The CRR bought the Vermont Valley Railroad, which later purchased the controlling interest in the M&WR from the estate of Alvin F. Sortwell (whose family had long been associated with it). Mellon then bought this interest from the Vermont Valley, bringing the M&WR into the B&M family in 1911.

It was a fertile time for the M&WR. A generous amount of butter traffic moved between Montpelier and Wells River, then south. Railroad Commissioners' reports of the time reflect a first-rate physical plant. And the quarry business was a virtual gold mine.

After the B&M took control of the M&WR, several interesting, if unrelated, events took place: hand-me-down B&M equipment began supplanting M&WR stock; the first grade crossing accident with a car occurred; and the *Green Mountain Express* was inaugurated in 1911 with an overnight sleeper connection to Boston, lasting until 1917 and the onset of the war.

Two corporate consolidations took place in 1913: the M&WR combined with the Barre Branch Railroad under the M&WR banner, and the East Barre & Chelsea (opened 1892—1.7 miles) combined with the Barre Railroad (which actually worked the quarries) to form the Barre & Chelsea Railroad, under M&WR control. Interestingly, no rails ever reached Chelsea.

The Mellon-controlled B&M ran into trouble. The New Haven began liquidating its B&M stock in 1914. In 1916 receivers were appointed, including one to administer the road's Vermont properties. The granite business collapsed in 1921—only 25% on the quarry workers remained employed. A year later regular passenger service to Barre ended.

In 1926 B&M General Manager (later President) Edwin S. French convinced his board that the parent should withdraw from local management while retaining ownership of the M&WR. He believed the only path to solvency was through local control and attention. French was named new president of the M&WR, and of the similarly befuddled St. Johnsbury & Lake Champlain, with joint offices in Montpelier.

Also in 1926 the local quarry companies decided to use their own locomotives and crews to operate, reducing revenue to the B&C. There were now only mixed trains plying the line, catering to mail and milk, and sometimes a few paying riders. Devastating flood damage on November 3 and 4, 1927 cost $284,000 in repairs. Montpelier-Barre was reopened November 16, while Montpelier-Wells River, so critical to transporting repair equipment to the ravaged Central Vermont, opened November 28. The CV didn't reopen until early February 1928.

The depression affected the road as it did all elsewhere; still, in 1932, the B&M and the M&WR cooperated on a new, fast service for overnight l.c.l. (less-than-carload) shipments to and from Boston. The B&C paid a dividend in 1937, none thereafter; there were modest losses in 1938, then a small profit in 1939. The 1930s witnessed the inevitable movement of the milk business to trucking, which could handle it with much greater flexibility.

Passenger revenues were dwindling as well. Where there had been four round trips to Wells River in 1928, there were but two in 1935, one of these a mixed-train. By 1936 all three trains were designated as mixed.

Further consolidation occurred in 1944 when the B&C

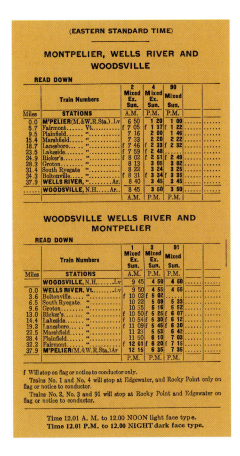

Left: *Montpelier & Wells River timetable from April 24, 1938, RWJ collection.*
Above: *Barre & Chelsea baggage check, Conway Scenic Railway collection.*
Above right: *Three Montpelier & Wells River tickets, Jack May collection.*

In Granite Country 127

Former B&M switcher No. 1172, Montpelier & Barre No. 29, has a respectable string of cars in Montpelier in October 1967. The Alco S-1 was built in 1949. In 1981 it would join the Washington County Railroad roster. David R. Sweetland photo.

acquired all M&WR holdings and took on the corporate identity. Following the absorption of the M&WR, B&C replaced seven of nine steam locomotives with three GE 600 hp, 70-ton diesels. The two newest steam locos, Nos. 5 and 6, both saddlebacks, were retained and eventually sold to the Rock Of Ages Quarry in 1948 and 1956, respectively. A consortium of three granite companies bought a controlling interest in B&C stock as a result of the postwar depression. In 1948 the road ended general merchandise pickup between Barre and Montpelier, and in 1951 the quarry train was dropped because of the severe decline in business. One of the remaining two mixed trains was discontinued in 1952, while the last lingered till January 1, 1956.

The B&C had suffered a long decline in business, and in 1956 the ICC authorized abandonment of the railroad. Just how unprofitable the Montpelier to Wells River segment was came to light in the abandonment petition: it had absorbed 40% of operating dollars while producing 5% of the revenue. And this with a mail contract!

Later in 1956, short-line magnate Samuel Pinsly agreed to buy the railroad with the proviso that he operate only the 14 miles from Montpelier through Barre to Graniteville. The Barre & Chelsea ran its last revenue train between Montpelier and Wells River on November 15.

For his new railroad, which Pinsly named the Montpelier & Barre, he bought two of the B&C diesels.

The trackage to Wells River was completely torn up by the following March, ironically at a time when scrap metal was fetching high prices. Much of the route is now Highway 302. Pinsly operated his first train to the quarries in January 1957. The M&B bought the CV's Barre Branch in 1958, combining the best of both routes in making a single new one.

The 1960s saw a continuing decline in traffic, with Vermont granite less in demand. The last profitable year was 1971; by 1977 the annual loss had grown to $104,000. Pinsly announced he would file to abandon in 1978. The Vermont Transportation Authority looked at how the situation might be salvaged. In 1979 there were four employees conducting once-a-week service.

The ICC approved the abandonment in March 1980. The state offered to pay up to $650,000 with the understanding that the Washington County Railroad Corporation (a banding together of the line's largest customers) would operate the road. There was much wrangling over the price; eventually it was settled at $740,000. The deciding factor was the commitment of Bombardier Ltd. of Canada to locate its railroad car assembly plant in Barre.

The Washington County Railroad began operations in December 1980 and continues today. A trackside spectator in Barre is just as likely to see a New York City subway car pass by on a flatcar as he is a shipment of grain.

128 **Green Mountain Rails**

Right: Russell F. Munroe visited the Rock of Ages Quarry on September 2, 1956 to photograph the road's two active steamers, 0-6-0 No. 27 and 0-6-2 No. 6.

Below: Twelve years later, in April 1967, No. 6—Hercules—has been cosmetically restored by Rock of Ages for display at the quarry. J. Emmons Lancaster photo.

Above right: RPO indicia, Montpelier Junction-Barre. RWJ collection.

Right: Montpelier & Barre snowplow 38 is not in good condition on October 24, 1967, yet its construction is fascinating. George W. Turnbull photo/Norton D. Clark collection.

In Granite Country

Above: A very typical marble train on the Clarendon & Pittsford is passing through Center Rutland on May 16, 1964. Russell F. Munroe photo. *Below:* A heavy blizzard in December 1961 has left a lot of snow on the ground and in the Springfield Terminal's switches. Alan Thomas found two railroad employees shoveling out the switches.

V
COUNTRY COUSINS
Clarendon & Pittsford
Hoosac Tunnel & Wilmington • Springfield Terminal

Like the proverbial country mouse so tellingly immortalized by Aesop, our three country cousins settled down comfortably to their bucolic way of life. These are solid country folk who never hankered for the pleasures of the city or its fast life, but who have been comfortable with the judicious pace of a rural existence. One of their number, the Springfield Terminal, would much later succumb to the temptations of a more worldly life, but at the time of our story she is content with her lot as the shortest of shortlines in Vermont, a sensible conveyor of freight and passengers between Springfield, Vermont, and a connection to the outside world seven miles hence in Charlestown, New Hampshire, where city cousin Boston & Maine stood ready with the promise of long-distance travel and its lures.

Indeed, so common-sense were the founders of the Springfield Terminal that they opted for electric operation when they incorporated in 1894. Springfield had been waiting for a railroad for fifty years, during which time seven different railroads had variously proposed routes to include Springfield, yet none was built. Had any of the schemes come to fruition, no doubt the railroad to Springfield would have been powered by steam, robbing us of this railroad's uniqueness.

Country cousin Clarendon & Pittsford led a life of nearly singular existence, that of freighting marble to nearby mainline rail connections. Eventually it recognized that a nice profit could be had by hauling other local commodities which lay hard by its tracks, but its main trade always remained the lucrative white rock for which Vermont was much envied.

Vermont Marble Company was such a closely knit family that its C&P rail employees were members of the marble worker's union rather than the usual railroad brotherhoods. Surely there is a streak of independence, perhaps even impudence, in such a stand, and yet this is surely worth admiration in an age when the railroad unions carried a mighty big stick indeed. This country cousin learned a few citified ideas about survival. She eventually married the Vermont son of city cousin Delaware & Hudson and still managed to keep her good name, sharing the considerable booty with her young neighbor and new landlord, Vermont Railway. Country folk learn early-on that life is chiefly about survival.

Our other country cousin, the Hoosac Tunnel & Wilmington, has, alas, gone to that great roundhouse in the sky. But in her day she lived a grand life and she had many, many friends. In a time before the automobile she enjoyed a land-office business in the tourist trade, for she indeed lived in some especially scenic country. And she saw the wisdom of catering to the railfan trade before anyone else, reaping not only goodwill but some worthwhile profits as well.

Our three country cousins, as unalike as they were from one another, shared the admirable quality of frugality and each seemed to know instinctively how to turn a dollar. Of course they were of their time, and their seasons have long since moved on. The Hoosac Tunnel & Wilmington has completely vanished. Springfield Terminal's rails are gone, its name usurped by another, a city cousin of suspect moral code. Although the Clarendon & Pittsford name is alive, most of the original track is gone, the marble business having been won over by the more versatile truck family.

But we remember our country cousins for the good-hearted, sensitive beings they were. We remember them for their can-do spirit and their stick-to-it tenacity, which imparted to them their quintessential Vermont character.

CLARENDON & PITTSFORD

The Green mantle which covers the mountains of Vermont and gave them their familiar name guards great wealth beneath the surface. Granite, talc, iron, slate, asbestos and many more resources are there, including marble—that white rock of monumental majesty.

Jim Shaughnessy
"White Rock and Green Hills"
The Railroad Enthusiast

The Vermont Marble Company created its own railroad in 1885 to move marble from the quarries to its finishing plants. Marble is so heavy, weighing a ton for every 11 cubic feet, that the advent of the railroad suited its purpose perfectly, and was far superior to earlier modes of shipping by horsepower on local roads. At first the tracks went from Center Rutland to West Rutland, and soon after to Proctor—Vermont Marble Company's main office and plant—about eight miles. Another nine miles of track were added in 1902, to Florence and, beyond that, to the Hollister Quarry. In 1911 the full 18-mile size was achieved with the addition of two tiny railroads: the Brandon & West Rutland and the Pittsford & Rutland. The resulting system connected with the Rutland Railroad at Florence, Proctor, Center Rutland, and Rutland, and with the Delaware & Hudson at West Rutland and Center Rutland. Until the early 1970s, C&P workers were all employees of Vermont Marble.

Early on, the C&P reaped extra revenues by hauling other commodities along its route, supplementing its lucrative marble trade. These included cement, coal, plywood, wire reels, and animal feed.

The little road saw yeoman service after the terrible 1927 flood, which hardly touched it because of the line's location high above Otter Creek. The C&P was a godsend to the Rutland, detouring the mail and passenger trains around ravaged trackage over its own tortuous curves and steep grades. Sometimes it took three of the C&P's 0-6-0 locomotives to get a train over, but it worked!

Passenger trains were run to move workers between plants and quarries until 1925, when the increased presence of the private auto made them unnecessary. Steam motive power consisted of a series of four- and six-wheel locomotives from Baldwin, Lima, and Alco. Dieselization came in 1945 with the arrival of two Whitcomb 44-tonners weighted down to 50 tons for improved traction on the steep grades.

The strike which closed the Rutland permanently in September 1961 brought an enormous increase in the

Left: *C&P No. 10 was one of two Whitcomb center-cab diesels delivered in March 1945. Originally black, they were soon painted traction orange. This is the crossing of the former Rutland Railroad at Center Rutland, seen on May 16, 1964. Note the hand-operated semaphores which controlled the interlocking. Russell F. Munroe photo.*

Right: *C&P acquired this GE 70-ton diesel from the Rutland after its demise, retaining the number 500. Here it is switching at West Rutland on October 3, 1967. George W. Turnbull photo/Norton D. Clark collection.*

Below: *C&P No. 10 is moving freight at Proctor on a cold and gray March 30, 1963. Russell F. Munroe photo.*

C&P's business until the evolution of the Vermont Railway in 1964. During these years the C&P worked valiantly to accommodate local shippers' needs, handling 500 to 600 cars per month, compared to 100 per month prior to the Rutland's demise. To assist with the extra chores, C&P bought the Rutland's 70-ton GE diesel.

In 1970 the C&P owned some 70 cars operated exclusively on the line, transporting various forms of the stone between the company's different operations. The road was bought by the Vermont Railway in 1972, by which time trucks were handling all the inter-plant marble shipments. In 1983, parent VTR arranged for the C&P to purchase the D&H branch to Whitehall, N. Y. Since separate corporate identity has been maintained, even today one can frequently see the C&P moniker backed by the VTR's resplendent carmine red paint scheme on no fewer than two road diesels and a switcher.

Ironically, it is C&P's Whitehall line which carries VTR's largest regularly scheduled freight—frequently with cars to and from the Green Mountain Railroad—six days a week to the Canadian Pacific/Delaware & Hudson interchange at Whitehall.

And so a distinguished old name lives on with a renewed purpose.

Country Cousins

HOOSAC TUNNEL & WILMINGTON

I took my place upon the fireman's seat after being duly introduced to him. There were so many gadgets that I really couldn't see how anyone could get them straight. It was very interesting to watch the engineer. As most of the track was down grade, he had to use the brake considerably. The escaping air made a very shrill noise when he applied it. The whistle was deafening when blown, and I was granted the privilege of ringing the bell. Another thing which interested me was the way in which the track seemed to appear out of nowhere when we rounded a curve.

When I climbed down at Hoosac Tunnel I decided that the best and most interesting place to ride on a train was the engine.

Bernice R. Beauregard
"Lady 'Enthusiast' Tells of HT&W Trip" [1934]
The Enthusiast

The Deerfield Valley Railroad Company was chartered in 1884 to link a profitable lumbering operation in southwestern Vermont with the Fitchburg Railroad at the Hoosac Tunnel. Its backers were four brothers from the Newton family of Holyoke, Massachusetts, who had suc- cessfully started a string of paper mills. A new source of pulpwood brought them to Readsboro, Vermont, and they soon envisioned a narrow-gauge railroad to replace the ox teams taking the pulpwood to the railhead. The first train ran on July 4, 1885, and a year later the Massachusetts portion of the road was organized as the Hoosac Tunnel & Wilmington. Six years later, in November 1891, the first scheduled train departed Wilmington, and in 1892 the entire 24 miles were designated as HT&W. A new dam created a mile west of Wilmington in 1893 spurred yet more profits in the lumber business.

An adjunct logging railroad was begun by the Deerfield Lumber Company in 1907, its tracks moving frequently to service new-found timber acreage. In its 15-year life, the peripatetic logging railroad served a total of more than 24 camps in the area.

The HT&W became standard gauge in 1913.

The New England Power Company bought the HT&W in 1920 and soon began construction of the giant Harriman Dam, requiring the relocation of the tracks further up the hillside above the river, since the valley would soon be flooded. Much to the annoyance of the power company, local public opinion forced it into restoring the line to Wilmington when the dam was completed. The new tracks were laid on top of the dam, and two switchbacks were needed to negotiate the new, higher right-of-way. These, coupled with the line's operating profile—tortuous curves and a rise of 800 ft. in its 24 miles—contributed to treacherous operating conditions.

The power company sold the road to local businessmen in late 1926; the following November it was severely damaged by the terrible November flood. New money was scraped together for the repairs, but passenger and mail service was permanently supplanted by a highway bus. Heavy spring rains in March 1936 washed away the trestle at Mountain Mills for the second time. Daunted by the task of rebuilding, the owners sold the HT&W to Samuel M. Pinsly—future owner of several New England short lines. Pinsly petitioned the ICC to abandon trackage north of Readsboro; the rails were removed and sold for scrap in the summer of 1937.

Pinsly rebuilt virtually the entire route as far as Readsboro after the devastating hurricane of September 1938, and eventually made the 11-mile line profitable. The road's first diesel arrived in 1949, a GE 44-tonner.

The building of the first U.S. nuclear power plant near Sherman Dam in Rowe, Massachusetts, brought about another rehabilitation of the line, followed by some very welcome business hauling construction materials for the plant between 1958 and 1960.

With the B&M's termination of passenger service west of Greenfield in early 1958, the HT&W ceased its highway bus service which had met trains at the Hoosac Tunnel Station. Back in May 1918 when the HT&W issued an expansive 28-page tourist brochure, there were three daily round-trips in the timetable—two mail-passenger trains as well as a freight. It was a beautiful region and the tourist trade flourished on the railroad, if only fleetingly.

The freight business dwindled to nothing during the 1960s, and Pinsly closed the line in July 1971. The HT&W's most famous hour came in 1934 with the inauguration of rail-enthusiast trips, the first in America, which continued for several years. Railfans were hardy folk then, and a derailment, which caused a two-hour delay on the southbound trip, was faced with humor:

> *After the excitement of the derailment had subsided, the passengers, with the prospect of spending the night there in their minds, set about to make themselves as comfortable as possible. Fortunately, the coach was equipped with a stove and with the supply of fuel on hand a fire was made which was decidedly welcome, driving off the sharp chill of the autumn air. The lighting system of the car was not in operation and a couple of lanterns provided the only means of illumination. The excursionists took the matter good-naturedly, however, and witticisms and singing were frequent. Stories of the reported presence of bears in that section of Southern Vermont failed to dampen their ardor.*

North Adams Evening Transcript

Opposite: *HT&W GE 44-tonner No. 15 is at Hoosac Tunnel Station on November 4, 1952, ahead of Travelers Express Company car 61, the company's only rolling stock. TEC was a Pinsly company, and the car was converted from a 40 ft. boxcar. This is the station where once HT&W trains interchanged passengers with the Boston & Maine. Donald S. Robinson photo.*

Above: *Cover of the 28-page promotional brochure published by the railroad in May 1918. It included 32 black & white photographs of scenic views and buildings, a railroad map, timetables from every conceivable rail connection to Wilmington (steamships up the Hudson River too!), and alluring descriptions of local hotels and taverns. RWJ collection.*

Above: *This is a typical late 1940s excursion on the HT&W, with the fans loaded into the gondolas at Hoosac Tunnel station. Whenever it rained on these excursions, patrons could be soaked to the skin. Possibly E-7 3800 heads the train to return them to Boston. Leon Onofri collection.*

Left: *The fascinating—and unique—double ended snowplow in October 1971. Today it is stored in good condition at the Valley Railroad in Essex, Connecticut.*

Above right: *This winter scene from February 1967 finds borrowed Claremont & Concord (another Pinsly-owned shortline) 70-ton No. 9 with four cars running alongside the Deerfield River. Two photos by H. Bentley Crouch.*

Right: *GE 44-tonner No. 16 is at Monroe Bridge, Massachusetts, in June 1970. Jack Armstrong photo.*

SPRINGFIELD TERMINAL

In 1952 I was moved to the freight sales office in the Concord, New Hampshire station and occupied the desk and office once used by the president of the Concord & Montreal Railroad. This era of my life, with its marble fireplaces, shiny brass cuspidors, and quiet elegance, soon came to an end. In January 1956 I was asked if I would be willing to assume new duties as general manager of the Springfield Terminal Railway Company and Cheshire Bridge Corporation in Springfield, Vermont. I was given a few days to think this over, but I could have given an affirmative answer right then and there!

Dwight A. Smith, Jr.
"I Ran New England's Last Country Trolley Line"
The Railroad Enthusiast

The Springfield Electric Railway Company was opened in July 1897 to connect the seven miles between Springfield, Vermont, and the Boston & Maine across the Connecticut River at Charlestown, New Hampshire. The road came under B&M control in January 1923, and was reorganized as the Springfield Terminal Railway.

Its Cheshire Bridge spanning the Connecticut River was a joint railroad and highway structure, some 500 ft. long, built in 1930. It's owner, the Cheshire Bridge Corporation (owned by Springfield Terminal), began in 1793 as Olcott's Ferry. In some later years the company's highway revenues from the bridge were greater than its rail freight income. On one occasion the local paper headlined "Cheshire Bridge Keeps Railroad Above Water."

Springfield was home to several important machine tool companies, accounting for significant outbound

138   Green Mountain Rails

```
SPRINGFIELD TERMINAL
RAILWAY COMPANY
JOHN WAHLEN, Gen. Mgr.
TIME TABLE
EFFECTIVE NOVEMBER 14, 1943
Eastern Standard Time
(Same as Eastern War Time)
Daily Schedule
Cars Leave      Arrive           Cars Arrive
Springfield     B. & M.          Springfield
 8:40 a. m.     9:18 a. m. South  10:35 a. m.
 8:40 a. m.    10:00 a. m. North  10:35 a. m.
12:15 p. m.    12:55 p. m. North   1:35 p. m.
12:30 p. m.     1:09 p. m. South   1:45 p. m.
 2:45 p. m.     3:23 p. m. North   4:20 p. m.
 2:45 p. m.     3:14 p. m. South   4:20 p. m.
 6:40 p. m.     7:18 p. m. North   8:30 p. m.
 7:10 p. m.     7:48 p. m. South   8:30 p. m.
10:45 p. m.    11:26 p. m. North  12:05 a. m.

        Sunday Schedule
 9:30 a. m.    10:09 a. m. North  10:40 a. m.
 3:10 p. m.     3:44 p. m. South   4:20 p. m.
 5:55 p. m.     6:40 p. m. North   7:10 p. m.
 8:00 p. m.     8:38 p. m. South   9:10 p. m.
11:00 p. m.    11:43 p. m. North  12:20 a. m.

Compliments of
COMSTOCK THE PRINTER
Charlestown, N. H.
```

Left: *Boston & Maine train 74 is arriving at the Charlestown-Springfield station behind Pacific 3696, purchased from the Lackawanna in 1943 and used mostly on the Connecticut River line. On the platform is a group of railfans who have enjoyed a trip into town on Springfield Terminal's steel trolley combine No. 16, built in 1926 by Niles. The tower in the distance is for the crossing tender (the freight house clerk). The station's order board was removed when it was realized that the sharp curve made it impractical. The infrequent orders were subsequently handled by the station agent.* **Above left:** *The ST did a good job meeting B&M trains. Only early morning trains weren't met; a taxi had to do. Conway Scenic Railway collection.* **Above right:** *No. 16 has pulled into the heart of ST's shops at Springfield, and the railfans are busy exposing film. Wooden combine No. 10, also built by Niles, is particularly popular today.* **Below:** *According to the church clock, it's 3:11 p.m., and No. 16 is about to depart to meet B&M No. 74 at 3:46 p.m. The Adnabrown Hotel was a noted landmark where railfans anticpated a fine lunch. Three photos summer 1946/Leon Onofri collection.*

Country Cousins

freight. The largest shipper for many years was Slack woolen goods, and there was also a foundry and a gas works. Incoming goods to service these industries included coal, coke, grain, petroleum products, building materials, pig iron, moulding sand, and unfinished steel.

Perhaps the ST's most famous alumnus was Edward S. French, who became the road's receiver in 1920, its president in 1925, and B&M president in 1930. French lived in Springfield, commuted to Boston on B&M's streamlined *Cheshire* (originally named *Flying Yankee*), and was a director of Springfield's Jones & Lamson Machine Co.

Passenger service was provided by three trolley combines painted in traction orange—wooden No. 10 and steel Nos. 16 and 17. Connections were provided for most B&M trains; only the overnight runs were not met. After this service was stopped in January 1947, steel combine No. 16 survived as a work car until the fall of 1956 when it went to the CERA Museum at Warehouse Point, Connecticut.

Springfield Terminal ordered a rebuilt GE 44-tonner to begin dieselization, and the former Sacramento Northern locomotive arrived in October 1956—soon lettered No. 1. To celebrate, local citizens were given free rides in an open gondola, and coffee and doughnuts in the new enginehouse, the former carbarn. The two steeplecab freight motors, Nos. 15 and 20, were sold to the Cornwall Railway Light & Power Company in Ontario, Canada. No. 20 exists in comfortable retirement at the Illinois Railroad Museum in Union, Illinois.

Business declined in the late 1950s and a succession of economies ensued. Tolls on the bridge were annulled during the early morning hours in December 1957 because the gate-keeper's wages exceeded his receipts. Crew sizes were reduced with union approval. Rate adjustments were made frequently to keep the line competitive. Piggyback service—the first shipment in Vermont—began in June 1959. Even postcards were sold for extra cash! After more than 20 years of service, No. 1 succumbed to mechanical failure, and the occasional business was handled by a leased B&M diesel.

The Springfield Terminal name became notorious in the mid-1980s, when Guilford Transportation Industries transferred the ST's liberal work rules to the rest of its system, throwing labor relations into havoc for years to come. The ST moniker appeared on Boston & Maine, Maine Central, and Delaware & Hudson locomotives.

Thus, ironically, the name of a small, unique, seven-mile rural railroad—once unknown to all but local citizens and a handful of interested railfans—has become well known as the name of a trans-New England system, synonymous with bare-bones operation and aggressive management.

On the original ST line, the last conventional freight train was handled in June 1984. Today the rails have been mostly removed, with the few remaining covered with asphalt at the crossings.

Left: Baldwin-Westinghouse No. 20 was a 50-ton 400 hp electric freight motor delivered in 1929. This is South Street in the center of Springfield in July 1956, three months before the close of electrification.

Right: Dieselization of the ST was accomplished with the purchase of an ex-B&M 44-tonner. Here is No. 1 in December 1961 slogging through wet snow dragging the company plow. Two photos by Alan Thomas.

Below: From the Official Railway Guide, *July 1935.*

Bottom: Headed for the junction in July 1975 with four cars, No. 1 passes by falls on the Black River. Ronald N. Johnson photo.

Springfield Terminal Railway Company
SPRINGFIELD, VT.

E. S. FRENCH, President . . . . Springfield, Vt.
JOHN WAHLEN, Superintendent . . .   "
L. A. PUTNAM, Assistant Treasurer . .   "

Electric Railway operating between Springfield, Vt., and Charlestown, N.H., 6.51 miles, connecting with all Boston & Maine R.R. passenger trains at Charlestown, N.H., except between 1 00 a.m. and 6 00 a.m.

Passenger, Freight and Express Service

February, 1935.

Country Cousins

Top: *The southbound Alouette is poised at Newport on September 3, 1956. Visible behind Canadian Pacific E-8 1801 are a CP RPO, a B&M stainless steel combine—made possible on this route because of excess capacity on its home Portland Division, a B&M "American Flyer" car, followed by a CP coach. Leon Onofri collection.* **Above:** *Grand Trunk train No. 17 is leaving Portland, Maine, behind CN 4-8-2 No. 6032 for its trip to Montreal. The 6032 was built by the Canadian Locomotive Company in 1924, one year after it built CN's first 4-8-2. T. J. Donahue photo.*

VI

CITY COUSINS

Boston & Maine • Canadian Pacific • Delaware & Hudson
Grand Trunk • Maine Central • Amtrak

Our six city cousins are a diverse lot indeed. A casual observer might wonder how they are related at all, so varied are their origins and dreams. Yet their common ground will become clear enough as the reader progresses through this chapter. Our city cousins are every bit as colorful as their country kin, and surely have done their part in the business successes of the region. The most extensive, the Canadian Pacific, is a major transcontinental railroad, with 114 miles in Vermont. The tracks of the smallest, the Maine Central, were built in Vermont in pursuit of just that kind of transcontinental traffic that cousin Canadian Pacific actually achieved. Similarly, the Grand Trunk was laid down in Vermont as a way of bringing lucrative Canadian freight traffic to Portland, Maine, for shipping. Though the GT accounted for only 35 miles of trackage in Vermont, the remote village of Island Pond and its denizens benefitted admirably from the presence of the railroad.

Across Vermont to the west, the Delaware & Hudson came a-courtin' for some of the wealth being created elsewhere in New England. It saw big opportunities in interchanging traffic with the Rutland, which at the time was still in an expansive mood, still hoping to be *the* link between eastern seaports and the Great Lakes. The D&H began buying significant chunks of Rutland stock. Two decades later, when it finally dawned on the D&H that these opportunities were not as profitable as they had surmised, divorce was inevitable. In an ironic twist of railroad intermarriage, the D&H in Vermont was ultimately acquired by the once tiny Clarendon & Pittsford, now puffed up with cash from daddy Vermont Railway, prosperous son of the late Rutland.

The Boston & Maine is probably the most infamous of Vermont's city cousins, having maintained in the state at one time much vaster estates than later hard times would permit. Almost everything now in the possession of the Canadian Pacific was once owned by the B&M, which found it was more than it could comfortably manage, and so sold it off in 1926. In more recent times an over-confident B&M found itself losing *all* its remaining Vermont trackage—from Brattleboro to Windsor—after a dispute with Amtrak, whose *Montrealer* was being inordinately slowed by poor track conditions, resulted in cousin Central Vermont acquiring these rails. Perhaps most surprising of all was the decision in Amtrak's favor by a Republican Supreme Court.

Amtrak's family lineage is a little unusual in that it is not a true cousin; it isn't really even a railroad—at least not in Vermont. But she travels here daily nontheless and deserves her brief pages in this volume.

If our city cousins are truly showing their age, they are still demonstrating an inherent tenacity deriving from their strong New England roots. Their survival insticts have taught them how to adapt to changing times to make it through.

Today there is quite a bit of railroad for sale in Vermont, including all the trackage of the Central Vermont and the Canadian Pacific. Perhaps it should be a time to worry, to contemplate whether *this* is maybe the final blow to a once vital and enterprising rail network.

Yet, looking over a century and a half of railroading in Vermont, we note that there have been hard times aplenty, with major adversities descending upon us regularly to jeopardize the status quo. Somehow clever individuals, with a flair for tinkering and a keen instinct on how to make it all work, always manage to appear to save the day. As in the case of the Rutland, sometimes their arrival is after midnight. Nonetheless they come.

City Cousins

BOSTON & MAINE

The Green Mountain Flyer has arrived from Rutland at Bellows Falls sometime in the late 1940s. Today's equipment is B&M Pacific 3703, Rutland wooden baggage car, B&M baggage-RPO, and B&M coach. In a few minutes the train will be on its way south into New Hampshire, over the B&M Cheshire Branch for Boston. The 3703 was built by Alco at Schenectady in 1923 and served the B&M for 30 years. Leon Onofri collection.

> *My eyes never beheld so fine a Country... I wish the Connecticut River flowed through Braintree... Nothing can exceed the Beauty, the Fertility of the Country.*
>
> John Adams
> Diary, June 8, 1771

When an empire-minded Boston & Maine swallowed the Boston & Lowell in 1887, one of the B&L's properties was the Connecticut & Passumpsic Rivers Railroad from Wells River, Vermont, to the Canadian border. Six years later, in 1893, the B&M leased the Connecicut River Railroad, including former Vermont Valley Railroad trackage between Brattleboro and Bellows Falls, and former Sullivan County Railroad trackage between Bellows Falls and Windsor. Hard times soon befell the much expanded B&M; New Haven Railroad control from 1907 to 1913 and bankruptcy in 1916 took their toll. Revenues were down and the railroad had excessive fixed-interest payments on leased properties, so in 1926 the line north of Wells River was leased to the Canadian Pacific.

Remaining Vermont holdings included the Brattleboro to Windsor segment, and a quarter-mile piece south of White River Junction to access the freight yard.

The Connecicut River line was once a very busy railroad. In Vermont the B&M double-tracked one mile north from Brattleboro, as well as 14.5 miles between Putney and Bellows Falls. The heavy rains and flooding in 1927 and 1936, which nearly wrecked New England's railroads, affected B&M's Vermont properties especially hard at Wells River, White River Junction, Bellows Falls, and Brattleboro.

Numerous colleges and universities along the Connecticut River helped to provide a healthy ridership for many decades, and famous name trains operating over the B&M included the *Montrealer-Washingtonian*, *Ambassador*, *Day White Mountains*, *Connecticut Yankee*, and *Overnighter*. Rutland's *Green Mountain Flyer* entered B&M rails at Bellows Falls, and we should not neglect to mention the *Cheshire*, B&M's articulated streamliner born in 1935 as the *Flying Yankee*, which for a number of years ran between White River Junction to Boston via Bellows Falls. Its frequent and most celebrated passenger was B&M President Edwin S. French who lived in Springfield, Vermont, and boarded the train at the Charlestown-Springfield station for the long commute to Boston. At least the train had the good grace to have a buffet aboard.

Seriously eroded passenger revenues lead the B&M to apply for abandonment of service in 1966. When this

Above: This February 1960 photo at White River Junction reveals an interesting aspect of B&M operations. During the winter and spring of both 1960 and 1961, the railroad used Budd RDCs for the Ambassadors as well as its Boston-Montreal and Boston-Berlin runs, resulting in the all-RDC consists shown here. Of the three trains, that on the left is the Montreal-Boston train (via CV). The center train with the illuminated headlight is the Springfield-Montreal train (via CV), while the right-hand train is its southbound counterpart. Passengers travelling beyond Springfield will change trains there. Interestingly, the third RDC on the center train has CP end markings. It was subsequently cut off by a switcher and coupled to a CP RDC from Boston; both went north over the CP to Montreal. The car at the far left is a B&M sleeper which spent days at White River Junction off the Montrealer-Washingtonian. A year later the B&M would rename two of its four stainless sleepers Dartmouth College I and II. Fred Matthews photo.

Right: A big storm has left major quantities of snow in the White River Junction yard. Here a crew of six aboard B&M GP-7 1560 and Jordan Spreader 3592 have made nice work of clearing the yard. The 1560 was built by EMD in 1950. The spreader was built by the O. F. Jordan Co. in 1923—the first of six bought by the B&M—then rebuilt and modernized in 1940. The spreaders were highly versatile maintenance-of-way machines, and depended on locomotive air for their operation. Photographed February 10, 1978 by Ronald N. Johnson.

City Cousins 145

B&M Pacific No. 3715 has an all-New Haven consist today on train No. 77, the Day White Mountains, between Charlestown and Claremont Junction on the Connecticut River Line. Second from the rear is a parlor car with a buffet for 1st class passengers. Probably it is Sunday since there is no RPO. For the purist, the train is in New Hampshire now but was in Vermont 15 minutes ago and will be again in half an hour. Leon Onofri collection.

occurred in October, the links between Boston and Montreal, and New York and Montreal were severed, resulting in the New Haven, Central Vermont, Canadian Pacific, and Pennsylvania Railroads annulling their contributions to these trains as well. Amtrak restored the *Montrealer* with much fanfare in 1972, then took it off in 1987 after the B&M allowed its tracks to deteriorate to a 10 mph running standard, unacceptable to Amtrak.

Freight traffic on the Connecticut River line began a steady decline after World War II and never recovered, so that by the late 1980s the B&M—and its owner, Guilford Transportation Industries—had lost the incentive to maintain it adequately. There was no profit here. Indeed, the B&M had tried selling the line to both the Central Vermont and the Canadian Pacific in the 1970s but neither was interested.

Amtrak sought a court remedy, which has been sustained by the Supreme Court; Amtrak bought the 49 miles from Brattleboro to Windsor, then immediately sold them to an eager Central Vermont, which rehabilitaed the track. Now Central Vermont had an uninterrupted mainline in New England, and the B&M's Vermont properties were down to 40 miles between White River Junction and Wells River, the yard at White River Junction, and some seven miles of double track (since single-tracked) near Pownal on the west end of the Fitchburg Division.

In 1993 Guilford announced its plan to sell its track from White River Junction to Wells River.

The Boston & Maine enjoyed some glorious times in Vermont, and these will be remembered as a valuable contribution to New England's railroad heritage.

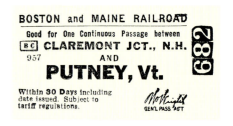

Above: Boston & Maine Railroad ticket, Claremont Junction to Putney. Jack May collection.

Right: A freight from Berlin has picked up two more diesels and is about to add more cars for its trip south to East Deerfield this bright January 1966 morning at White River Junction. On the point are B&M GP-9 1741, GP-9 1825 (the upgraded 1725), GP-7 1568, and GP-9s 1715 and 1743. Note the two cross-country skiers just beyond the tank cars, curiously inspecting the scene. Ronald N. Johnson photo.

CANADIAN PACIFIC

The one pattern of fishing unique to Vermont is at Newport on the southern shores of Lake Memphremagog.... Whoever sees the first crack in the ice dashes for his rod, passing the word en route, and within an hour half the city is on the railroad bridge which spans the southern tip of the lake.... Several years back a sportsman, in the backlash of a cast, hooked the ear of a brakeman on a passing train. Forthwith the Canadian Pacific dismissed all fishermen from the bridge and for a time it looked as though the angling would have to be done from the less advantageous banks of the Clyde; but the railroad company eventually relented, declaring an armistice, and excluded only the fly-casters.

W. Storrs Lee
The Green Mountains of Vermont

Today's Canadian Pacific in Vermont was originally chartered in 1835 as the Connecticut & Passumpsic Rivers Railroad, envisioned as part of a through route south from Montreal to both Boston and New York. Six New England railroads provided financial backing for this route—Boston & Maine; Boston, Concord & Montreal; Concord Railroad; Manchester & Lawrence; Nashua & Lowell; and Northern of New Hampshire—since all would benefit from its gateway to the north. The first 60 miles were completed in 1850 from White River Junction—where it connected with the Vermont Central and the Northern of New Hampshire—to St. Johnsbury. It reached the Canadian border at North Derby Junction, another 50 miles, in 1863. From there the plan had been to link up with the Stanstead, Shefford & Chambly, but Vermont Central's J. G. Smith thwarted this move by buying the SS&C himself. Instead, the Passumpsic road linked up with the Massawippi Valley Railway, which ran from the border to Lennoxville, just south of Sherbrooke, for an across-the-platform connection with the 5 ft. 6 in. gauge Grand Trunk.

Although this new connection provided business with Quebec and eastern Canada, there was still the Passumpsic's desire for Montreal trade. The solution was to build the Missisquoi & Clyde Rivers Railroad 33 miles west from Newport to the border above Richford, where it would meet the South Eastern Counties Junction Railway, coming down from West Farnham, Quebec. With this accomplished by February 1873, the Passumpsic had its coveted route to Montreal.

But not without enormous costs, and eventually the Passumpsic road lost control of the Montreal connections. The Missisquoi & Clyde Rivers became the Newport & Richford. The Passumpsic came under Boston & Lowell control in 1887, and later under the Boston & Maine in 1893.

The Canadian Pacific first became a presence in

Left: *Canadian Pacific's Lyndonville shops, shown here in 1946, were the oldest on the road's eastern lines; they were torn down soon after the CP dieselized in Vermont in 1949.*

Right: *Orleans had a picturesque depot set amidst lovely grounds. Sandy Worthen was riding the Alouette in 1946 when he made both photos.*

Below: *Canadian Pacific Railroad ticket, Newport to Montreal. Jack May Collection.*

Bottom: *The northbound Alouette is arriving at Newport on July 10, 1954. According to photographer Sandy Worthen, "In the days of steam here, northbound trains ran into the station on the Quebec Central track on the east side of the station, so that the locomotive could take water and immigration inspection could be carried out. The train then reversed across the Main Street crossing to the switch for the main line to Richford and Montreal."*

City Cousins

Vermont in 1926 when it leased the Passumpsic (north of Wells River) and the Newport & Richford from the B&M. The line north from Newport to Sherbrooke came under CP's subsidiary, the Quebec Central. Twenty years later the Canadian Pacific purchased these properties outright from the B&M in 1946.

Because CP's Montreal-Wells River Division was among the road's first to be completely dieselized—in 1949—color photography of steam is so rare that the author despaired of ever finding any at all. It was only at the eleventh hour that material appeared.

As elsewhere in rural New England, through traffic on the CP declined gradually from the 1960s through the 1980s. After a brief surge of through traffic with the Boston & Maine in the late 1980s, business has again reverted to just local service. Now the CP routes this through traffic by way of its Montreal to Albany and Binghamton line from its recent acquisition, the Delaware & Hudson. Indeed, the CP proposes to abandon its Vermont line between Newport and Wells River. Possibly one of the local short lines will acquire the property.

For several decades the CP hosted two famous Boston-Montreal passenger trains. The *Alouette* was a day train featuring a buffet-parlor-observation car at the rear, while the *Red Wing* was a leisurely overnight train with Pullman sleeper service. Both plied the B&M's colorful Lake Winnepesauke route until 1954—the former Boston, Concord & Montreal—when it was closed north of Plymouth. Thereafter they made the trip via White River Junction on the old Northern Railroad route. Both trains were often pulled by the handsome maroon and gray CP E-units purchased for this purpose. The *Alouette* name was dropped in 1956, with service then covered by Budd RDCs from both the CP and the B&M. The *Red Wing* made its last trip in October 1959. Just a single daytime round trip survived until that too was deleted in January 1965.

In 1993 a Monday through Friday freight operated between Montreal and Newport, while a local freight journeyed from Newport to Richford for a feed company there. A Newport-St. Johnsbury round trip operated two days a week in the summer, sometimes venturing further south to Barnet and East Ryegate for paper mill needs. In the winter the service was increased to three times a week to serve the Lyndonville Gas Co.

The railroad scene in New England is as mercurial as its weather. Should a short line company assume operation of CP rails in Vermont, it could continue as a viable enterprise. And for those of us who believe in the efficacy of the passenger train, we can dream about riding this majestic route yet again on some future day.

Left: Preston Johnson was at Bradford, Vermont, on September 13, 1955 to make this photo of Hap Magoon hooping up the orders to the engineer on Canadian Pacific RS-3 8453.

Right: Canadian Pacific certainly knew how to dress up a Budd Car. This is RDC-2 No. 9113 at White River Junction on May 30, 1963. Russell F. Munroe photo.

Center right: The CP headquarters at St. Johnsbury was a formidable structure. This is December 29, 1965. John F. Kane photo.

Below right: Sandy Worthen photographed the Lyndonville depot as he passed by on the rear observation platform of the Alouette in 1946.

Below: The RPO indicia from a Newport & Springfield U. S. Mail car. RWJ collection.

Bottom: Quebec Central Railway ticket, Newport to Beebe Jct. Jack May collection.

City Cousins

Left: *CP freight extra 4010 is southbound on the B&M at Fairlee behind Alco FAs in October 1959. Preston Johnson photo.*

Below: *CP RS-18 8729 and RS-3 8446 are near White River Junction on May 2, 1965. Russell F. Munroe photo.*

Bottom: *Dwight A. Smith photographed CP 2-8-2 No. 5146 in July 1957 at Derby on the Quebec Central. The locomotive was built in 1913 by the Montreal Locomotive Works.*

152   Green Mountain Rails

Top: We're looking across the Clyde River towards the B&M-CP-Quebec Central depot at Newport. A passenger train behind CP steam is having its head end serviced. The steamer at the far left appears to be on an adjacent track, rather than a double-header. Sandy Worthen photo.

Above: The Alouette has slowed for its arrival at Wells River on July 15, 1950, with classic CP E-8 No. 1800. Note the conductor on the steps of the second car. Preston Johnson photo.

Right: This elegant 1888 brochure harks back to an era when the railroads had a virtual monopoly on vacations and recreation. Sandy Worthen collection.

154   Green Mountain Rails

Upper left: With the imposing Jay Peak in the distance, CP train 904 is at Newport Center following the great blizzard in March 1993. The power is CP RS-18u 1866 and C-424 4241. Mike Confalone photo.

Left: Here's train 904 on August 19, 1972, near the summit at Sutton, Vermont, behind CP RS-18 8760, RS-3 8436, RS-10 8572, RS-3 8413, and RS-10 8563.
John F. Kane photo.

Above: Ronald N. Johnson made this stunning photo of CP train 937 rounding Lake Memphramagog on September 29, 1978, behind GP-35 5015 and C-424s 4215 and 4249.

Right: It was 18° below zero this February dawn in 1992 at the Newport engine terminal when Mike Confalone made this time exposure of CP RS-18m 1801.

City Cousins 155

DELAWARE & HUDSON

On a bright October day, the weather so mild that natives termed it June-like in spite of a snowfall three days earlier, your author took himself to the railroad station of the Delaware & Hudson... A word or two on the coach that you may follow me more vividly on my eighty-eight mile jaunt. Number 277 is a wooden car painted D&H green, with stoves in diagonal corners (burning D&H anthracite of course!), green plush seats that come only up to your back in a comfortable manner and not over the top of your head, electric lights, a water fountain but no other running water. The cubicles at the end of the car marked "men" and "Women" proved to be "phone booths of the backyard variety."

Howard Nelson Gutherie
"The Fun Farm"
The Railroad Enthusiast

The Delaware & Hudson took its railroad operation to Vermont in June 1870 when it leased trackage built 20 years earlier.

The first railroad to be built west from Rutland was the Rutland & Washington—originally envisioned to connect with other roads at Whitehall, New York. But the organizers decided that greater wealth awaited them with a different route, so they turned south at Castleton, public opinion notwithstanding. Service was opened the ten miles from Rutland to Castleton in October 1850, then to Eagle Bridge, New York in March 1852. Trains between Rutland and Albany began operation in July 1853.

Another company, the Rutland & Whitehall, was subsequently chartered to provide the line abdicated by the Rutland & Washington. In an economy gesture, the new road used the existing tracks between Rutland and Castleton. Service began in November 1850, providing a through link between New York City and Montreal.

Also in November 1850 the Rutland & Whitehall was leased to the Saratoga & Washington (the New York segment of the Whitehall line). Both roads later came under control of the Rensselaer & Saratoga in June 1865. This company was in turn leased to the much larger Delaware & Hudson in June 1871. The D&H designated the line to Whitehall its Saratoga Division, that to Eagle Bridge its

D&H "Mother Hubbard" No. 819 is switching at Fort Edward, New York, in preparation for taking a freight to Rutland. The loco was built by Alco in 1906, then rebuilt and renumbered by the D&H in 1926. She was scrapped in 1951. Leon Onofri collection.

Above: *Castleton station as seen in October 1961. We look east to Rutland, with the line to Salem, New York, in the foreground, and that to Fort Edward left of the depot. RWJ photo.* ***Below:*** *Baldwin RF-16 Sharks Nos. 1216 and 1205 lead a freight at Granville, New York, on August 11, 1976. The two diesels were the last operating RF-16s. Originally delivered December 1951 and January 1952 to the New York Central, they went to Penn Central in 1968, then to associate Mononghahela Railway. The D&H acquired them in 1972 under President Bruce Sterzing and overhauled them at Watervliet shops. After D&H they went to the Escanaba & Lake Superior Railroad. Albert G. Hale photo.*

Rutland & Washington Division.

When the D&H acquired these Vermont lines in 1871, business was excellent. Each of the two divisions was served by four daily passenger trains to Rutland, and there was a booming trade in slate. Later the D&H would benefit from the thriving marble business on the Clarendon & Pittsford.

For two decades the D&H was interested in controlling the Rutland as a way of tapping into lucrative New England traffic. Stock was gradually acquired over several years until a controlling interest was accomplished in 1887. By 1899, however, the D&H thought better of the idea, and sold its Rutland stock to local banker Percival W. Clement.

The D&H maintained its own right-of-way into Rutland and its own five-track yard until heavy flooding washed out both its and the Rutland RR's bridge in 1947. When the Rutland rebuilt its own bridge, the D&H acquired trackage rights into the city.

D&H's passenger ridership on its two Vermont division weakened sufficiently that these trains were dropped in June 1934. The automobile had long since caught the fancy of local citizens. The milk shipments formerly handled on passenger trains were now carried on freights into the 1950s until refrigerated trucks proved more efficient.

The D&H brought diesels to its Vermont lines in 1946 with RS-2s.

A single daily freight—called the "Hill Job"— worked the line to Rutland in the 1960s and 1970s, detouring onto the line south from Castleton when necessary. The D&H eventually abandoned the Rutland & Washington Division; rails were lifted in 1990.

The Vermont Railway caused its subsidiary, the Clarendon & Pittsford, to purchase the Rutland-Whitehall portion of the D&H Saratoga Division in 1983, with considerable resources going into the deteriorating line's renewal.

Ironically, it is this part of the Vermont Railway which today accounts for its most significant tonnage and revenues.

Below and Below far right are two excerpts from the Delaware & Hudson pages of the 1893 Official Guide. RWJ collection.

It is cold and bright this January 30, 1994 morning as Clarendon & Pittsford's Whitehall to Rutland daily freight catches the early sun just west of Rutland. Typically this train makes its way under the cover of darkness. Today's power is Vermont Railway GP-38-2 No. 202, C&P GP-38 203, and C&P SW-1500 502. This former Delaware & Hudson trackage is Vermont Railway's biggest revenue producer. Mike Confalone photo.

Rutland...............	0	†6 25 A.M	†10 25 A.M.	1 15	†4 10 P.M	†5 45
Centre Rutland...............	1	6 28 ″	10 29 ″	1 19	4 15 ″	5 56
West Rutland........	4	6 33 ″	10 34 ″	1 24	4 23 ″	6 05
Castleton...................	10	6 41 ″	10 45 ″	1 36	4 33 ″	6 25
Hydeville..............	13	6 46 ″	10 50 ″	1 42	4 38 ″	6 35
Fair Haven...............	15	6 49 ″	10 53 ″	1 46	4 41 ″	6 41
Whitehall............... arr.	23	7 05 A.M.	11 10 A.M.	2 05	4 55 P.M.	7 10

City Cousins

GRAND TRUNK

In a vivid depiction of why the location is called Island Pond, we're looking southeast during the 1954 July 4 weekend. Arthur E. Mitchell photo.

For generations of New Englanders, the Grand Trunk Railway was the symbol and model of a "great way to run a railway." It was an ambitious scheme to eliminate the U. S.-Canadian border as a barrier to trade and commerce and build a high speed conveyor of goods. It was a pioneer in using the finest and latest equipment, and its locomotives were kept in first-class condition, ever worthy of that second look of admiration and awe. The management encouraged the employees to share in the "Great Grand Trunk Dream" and their loyalty was ever-present through all the railway's triumphs and tribulations. These Grand Trunk men were former Maine fishermen, New Hampshire woodsmen, Vermont farmers, British supervisors, and Canadians from the Eastern townships to British Columbia. Its very name—Grand Trunk—denotes a famous old highway in British Imperial India.

John Carbonneau
Grand Trunk Heritage

A visionary entrepreneur named John Alfred Poor believed that Portland's future glory lay in the creation of a railroad between Portland and Montreal. He saw Portland capitalizing on Montreal's wealth as a seaport for wheat and grain from the west, especially during the winter when the St. Lawrence River was frozen, denying Montreal its ocean access. That Portland was the nearest seaport, and that it was also closest to England of its rival American ports were both in Poor's favor.

So convincing was Poor's zeal that he convinced enough Portland backers to get the Atlantic & St. Lawrence Railroad started. Poor was a believer in the future of Maine and eventually would promote five other railroad projects in the state. With difficulty he got a charter for the Atlantic & St. Lawrence. When he learned that Boston interests were seeking to turn the Montreal Board of Trade against his own plan, he braved a perilous horseback trip to Montreal in the dead of the 1845 winter to make his case. He had the important support of Sir Alexander Tilloch Galt, who ran the British American

Land Company, holder of 747,000 acres of land in the Quebec eastern townships. It was on this land that Canadian backers agreed to build the St. Lawrence & Atlantic south from Montreal.

Despite enthusiastic support from Maine citizens, and a jubilant ground-breaking celebration in July 1846, progress was was slow and disappointing. Engineering difficulties mounted, costs soared, and subscribers were recalcitrant in their payments. Excessive rain, marshy soil, employee accidents, and labor disputes all contributed to runaway costs. By August 1849 only 47 miles of the 165 to the Canadian border were completed, at 60% of the total line's estimated cost.

The Maine Legislature gave assistance, and the city of Portland made three loans totaling $2 million. For the next four years the road slogged on.

Tracks to Island Pond, Vermont, were completed in February 1853, when the Atlantic & St. Lawrence called it quits 16 miles from the border at Norton, having spent just over $6 million to get there, more than double the original estimate. Fortunately an agreement had been reached with a sister road, the St. Lawrence & Atlantic, to build here from Canada, and on July 18 the first train ran through from Montreal to Portland. Both component roads were leased to the Grand Trunk of Canada the prior July 1.

Interestingly the builders chose a wide, 5 ft. 6 in. gauge to achieve maximum traction (isolating it from Boston competition and interchange), but the realities of commerce caused a change in 1874, when between midnight and 7:00 a.m. on September 25 and 26, the entire line was converted to standard gauge. Just imagine the labor force to accomplish this—and the coffee and pastry!

Portland benefitted well from the commerce the railroad engendered, though it would never rival Boston as a seaport. Poor's dream really had come true, yet it was seasonal success. In the warm months, considerable tonnage still moved out of Montreal by water, and business along the line was sparse indeed. Island Pond was created in the middle of the route in 1853—inside the town of Brighton with its scarcely 300 local farmer residents—and became a prosperous railroad town overnight. It was active for decades as a division point, and its easy access to Portland, Lewiston, Sherbrooke, and Montreal stimulated a healthy sophistication among its citizenry. With its spectacular lake and magnificent brick station, Island Pond could quite possibly be the single most beautiful railroad town ever created in North America.

The Grand Trunk became seriously overextended in its bid to become a continental rail entity to the Pacific, at the deep harbor port of Prince Rupert, British Columbia, and it faltered. The Canadian government took over the troubled line along with several others in 1919, amalgamating them into the Canadian National System in 1923. This change spelled the end of a once immense grain business for Portland, since such traffic was now routed to port at Saint John, New Brunswick, and Halifax, Nova Scotia. Canada wanted the revenues.

Other commodities, such as meat and dairy products dwindled quickly in the next years, with service facilities along the line shrinking away.

In contrast to the swelling winter traffic caused by the frozen St. Lawrence River, summer passenger trains became highly popular with Canadians and Vermont and New Hampshire residents taking their pleasure at Maine beaches. The most famous, *The Maine Coast Special*, went via Grand Trunk from Montreal to Yarmouth Junction, via Maine Central to Portland, then via Boston & Maine to Scarboro Beach, Old Orchard Beach, Biddeford, and Kennebunk. The train was sadly killed off by the up-and-coming automobile after the 1939 season. Still, daily trains Nos. 16 and 17 frequently ran with extra sections in the summer months. Management lost the U. S. Mail contract in the mid-1950s, then, with passenger losses mounting, regular year-round service ended on Labor Day 1960. Only summertime weekend trips continued, by court order, until 1967, the very end of passenger service.

City Cousins 161

In 1989 Canadian National sold the section between Norton and Portland to Emons Holdings Corporation of Pennsylvania, who renamed it the St. Lawrence & Atlantic. The new road operates a small but profitable freight business, using several old ex-GT GP-9s and three leased GP-40s, with a daily eastbound originating at Island Pond in the morning, and a daily westbound arriving there from Danville Junction, Maine, in the evening. Lumber, for decades a crucial enterprise to Island Pond and the line, is again an important rail commodity there.

The Grand Trunk was one of Vermont's shortest rail lines—scarcely 30 miles in the far corner of the Northeast Kingdom. Its real honor was being North America's first international railway.

Left: The brick depot at Island Pond has a castle-like quality. It was built in 1904 and still stands today.

Right: Switcher 7530 is busy with yard chores this glorious July 4 weekend in 1954. Business looks very good, indeed. The 0-6-0 switcher was built in 1919 and is close to retirement. Two photos by Arthur E. Mitchell.

Below left: We're looking across the yard to the island on a drizzly June 1, 1955. Judging from the rust on the front of 3709, she's been sitting here a while. One year later the Grand Trunk was completely dieselized, although the 3709 wasn't scrapped until November 1959.

Below right: A way freight arrives from west of Island Pond. Two photos by T. J. Donahue.

162   Green Mountain Rails

City Cousins 163

Above: No. 7530 is backing past the ice house at Island Pond in early July 1954. Note that the Swift refrigerator car is being iced by an employee working atop the bright red car. Arthur E. Mitchell photo. *Below:* St. Lawrence & Atlantic train 394 is passing through Island Pond in January 1992 behind mixed power: CV GP-9 4445, GATX SW-1500 9626 (originally Reading), and GATX GP-40 3717 (originally Baltimore & Ohio). The village beyond looks inviting indeed. Mike Confalone photo.

Right: St. Lawrence & Atlantic train 393 is at Island Pond on February 27, 1993 behind Canadian National GE Dash 8-40cm 2422.

Below: Portland to Island Pond RPO indicia. Courtesy of Howard F. Moulton.

Bottom: The winter of 1993 saw the beginning of a new ski train operation on the St. Lawrence & Atlantic between Portland and Bethel, Maine, called the Sunday River Silver Bullet Ski Express. Here the attractive train is deadheading east at Brighton, Vermont, on December 12, 1993 behind freshly painted GP-9 1764. The inaugural run took place on Monday, December 20, 1993. Two photos by Mike Confalone.

City Cousins

MAINE CENTRAL

Over the Connecticut into Lunenburg we are surprised to find a large abandoned engine house with no apparent reason for its existence, until Conductor C. W. Raymond explains that this was the terminus of the old Portland & Ogdensburg Railroad and the St. Johnsbury & Lake Champlain. Brakeman A. J. Parent has been predicting heavy rain for some time back and it becomes a reality as we pull into Gilman. All the work here has to do with the one industry of the town, a huge paper mill, and from the remarks of the trainmen it is plenty tonight. Parent profanely states that all the messes come on stormy nights, and this is a daisy. After a long period of switching, during which we talk and listen to the rain beat on the windows, we are ready to go. The trainmen come in and change their soaking outer garments, and Parent unlimbers a well-oiled and magnificent vocabulary that covers everything from the weather to taxes. I feel that I could tackle about any tough job with a man who could swear like that.

Artemas O. Wilkins
"A Day With a Way Freight in the Mountains"
The Railroad Enthusiast

We noted in Chapter III, St. Johnsbury and Lake Champlain, that it was entrepreneurs from Portland, Maine—looking to link their seaport with the Great Lakes—who enabled the building of the Portland & Ogdensburg Railroad. East of the Connecticut River, construction had reached as far west as Fabyans when the Maine Central leased it in 1888. The MEC soon completed the connection to the Essex County Railroad (part of the StJ&LC) on the west bank of the Connecticut at Lunenburg, Vermont. The Essex County was leased by the MEC in 1902, completing the parent road's Mountain Division from Portland to St. Johnsbury.

The second and more northerly arm of the Mountain Division was begun in 1887 by lumber baron George Van Dyke, who saw railroads as the most efficient way of getting his product to market. He envisioned a 108-mile line north from Quebec Junction to Lime Ridge, Quebec, and subsequently received four separate charters—one in New Hampshire, two in Vermont, one in Quebec—to build the line. He began in the middle of the route at North Stratford where his railroad could connect with the Grand Trunk, leaving the southern half until later. Construction began in August 1887, and the last spike was driven at Beecher Falls, Vermont, in January 1889, connecting with the Hereford Railway which had been abuilding simultaneously south from Lime Ridge. The Hereford—later known affectionately as the *Raspberry Branch* for its berry shipments—connected with both the Canadian Pacific and the Quebec Central in Canada.

Van Dyke didn't finish his road, but left that task to the Maine Central which leased the above completed properties in May 1890. By late February 1891 the MEC had completed the southern connection to Quebec Junction.

For the curious, here are the component roads which Van Dyke chartered, from south to north:
1. Upper Coos ("ko-us") Railroad, New Hampshire (first section)—14.5 miles.
2. Coos Valley Railroad, Vermont—12 miles.
3. Upper Coos Railroad, New Hampshire (second section)—27 miles.
4. Upper Coos Railroad, Vermont—1.5 miles to Beecher Falls.
5. Hereford Railway—53 miles in Quebec to Lime Ridge.

In the heyday of the great summertime mountain resorts, there was considerable passenger business on the Mountain Division, including a through parlor car from Boston to Beecher Falls. Even after the automobile became popular, the Maine Central operated a daily Portland-Beecher Falls train.

After the lumber business within easy reach of the railroad dropped off in the early 1920s, the MEC cancelled its lease of the Hereford and abandoned its trackage in Canada. Further cost cutting measures on the MEC in 1933 included removing all but a daily mixed train between Lancaster and Beecher Falls. The Ethan Allen Furniture Company located there long accounted for sustained freight business.

Sleeping cars on the Portland-St. Johnsbury-Montreal route saw their last service in 1929. After that, Portland-St. Johnsbury was served by a daily round-trip with a baggage car, railway mail car, and a single coach. Fortunately the freight business remained strong in the 1930s with pulpwood, milk, and manufactured products, and World War II increased it even more.

Nineteen miles of the line between Coos Junction and North Stratford—much of it in Vermont—were taken up in summer 1949 as an economy move. Alternate routing was arranged on the B&M and the Grand Trunk. Though the Mountain Division was dieselized in 1950, the Beecher Falls branch kept its steam through the following May.

Pulpwood traffic increased at Beecher Falls while other local traffic on this line and that to St. Johnsbury declined in the mid-1950s recession. Bridge traffic was still

Train YR-1 is leaving St. Johnsbury bound for Portland on June 23, 1978, behind five diesels. In the lead are GP-38s 260 and 255, while further back is RS-11 801. Ronald N. Johnson photo.

168   Green Mountain Rails

Left: Maine Central freight YR1 has stopped for orders at Gilman on July 8, 1977, with GP-38 257 on the point.

Below left: The same train passes through Miles Pond on July 29, 1983 and gets enthusiastic waves from vacationers. Two photos by Ronald N. Johnson.

Right: At St. Johnsbury, Maine Central E-7 709 will soon be hitched up to its passenger train for the return trip to Portland. Arthur E. Mitchell photo. The classic diesel was sold to Kansas City Southern in 1963.

Below: Maine Central Railroad tickets to Lunenburg and Miles Pond. Jack May collection.

Bottom: Ronald N. Johnson beautifully captured the fall colors at East St. Johnsbury on September 26, 1979 as YR1 came through behind U-18-B 401.

Above: Beecher Falls experienced a 20° below zero temperature on February 15, 1975. The freight depot still sports the original blue enamel sign, as well as some mighty hefty icicles. ***Below right:*** On the same day Maine Central GP-7 564 departs south with five MEC boxcars and a buggy for its journey over the Mountain Division to Portland. Two photos by Ronald N. Johnson. ***Above right:*** Maine Central 2-6-0 No. 367 is about to depart Beecher Falls with the mixed train for Bartlett, New Hampshire, on July 16, 1950. It carries milk cars destined for Boston. The station's order board still has two blades, even though service north of here ended nearly 30 years earlier. The locomotive was built by Alco at its Providence, Rhode Island, shops in 1906. Preston Johnson photo.

robust. The passenger coach was taken off the Beecher Falls mixed train in April 1955, and the daily Portland-St. Johnsbury train ended in April 1958. In its last years it enjoyed the luxury of a streamlined combine, available because of declining traffic on the Boston-Bangor route for which it was built.

Local traffic on the Mountain Division continued its decline from the 1960s through the 1980s; nonetheless the MEC still profited from substantial bridge traffic, serviced by a daily freight. The Beecher Falls branch was severely damaged by flooding in the spring of 1973. The MEC tried to abandon the line, citing low revenues and high restoration costs. Rebuffed by the courts, it was forced to reopen the line 17 months later. After further consideration, the MEC was allowed to sell the branch to the state of New Hampshire. MEC made its last trip to Beecher Falls in February 1977. In March the newly-formed North Stratford Railroad took over operation of the branch north to Beecher Falls.

Increasing derailments on the St. Johnsbury line prompted the New England Regional Commission to put $500,000 toward roadbed and crossing improvements.

The MEC was sold to U. S. Filter Corporation in December 1980, and again in June 1981 to Guilford Transportation Industries. Guilford favored a western route via its two other properties—Boston & Maine and Delaware & Hudson—and traffic was increasingly moved off the Mountain Division. Guilford negotiated an alternate interchange with the Canadian Pacific, and the last through train ran on the division in September 1983. The Lamoille Valley Railroad (see Chapter III) acquired the tracks from St. Johnsbury to Whitefield, New Hampshire in 1984, operating it as the Twin State Railroad. In 1989 it came under new management, the newly-created New Hampshire & Vermont, which also acquired B&M branches from Woodsville to Berlin and Groveton, New Hampshire.

Today a local freight works west from Whitefield daily to a paper company in Gilman, Vermont, going all the way to St. Johnsbury several times each week for interchange with the CP.

While the famous and rugged portion of Maine Central's Mountain Division through Crawford Notch pines away unused, its Vermont brother is still operational and profitable in today's difficult rail market.

City Cousins 171

AMTRAK

The northbound Montrealer *can usually be photographed in Vermont only during summer's long days.* **Above:** *We're at East Alburgh on September 1, 1978 as the train is headed by E-8 496 and F-40PH 212.*

Right: *On July 7, 1977, the photographer created this fine portrait of the* Montrealer *from a hill above Montpelier Junction. Two photos by Ronald N. Johnson.*

> *June in Vermont is a jewel... nothing, absolutely nothing, compares with a fine morning in June... If everything clicked... you'd hear the distinctive note of an Amtrak F40PH blowing for crossings in the distance, and then, much sooner than it seemed possible, the northbound* Montrealer *would smash by in a silver blur, and be gone.*
>
> Benjamin B. Bachman
> "The Vermont Year"
> *Trains*

Amtrak—the National Railroad Passenger Corporation—is the youngest of Vermont's City Cousins. Really, it is more like a second cousin because here it owns no track of its own, making its way through the state on Central Vermont iron. Indeed, given that it has only a single daily train, that it's operation was interrupted for two years while track was upgraded by CV, and that its consist was recently downgraded in a budget trimming exercise, it is perhaps better thought of as a second cousin, twice removed.

No matter, Amtrak's *Montrealer* is still Vermont's only mainline passenger train today, providing access to both Montreal and New York, and several smaller cities in between. The train still carries college students and skiers, and local denizens looking for a night's rest as they travel in and out of the state. Perhaps we should have said *part* of a night's rest, given the train's nocturnal schedule. White River Junction departure times were 10:50 p.m. southbound, and 5:10 a.m. northbound, in the autumn of 1993. The diner, lamentably, is gone, but there is a snack service and first-class passengers are entitled to "tray meals."

We speak of the *Montrealer's* history in more detail in the Central Vermont chapter. Yet we would like to remember here as well that its southbound component was for many years called the *Washingtonian*, this appellation appearing briefly in Amtrak's recreation of the train in September 1972. Vermont was without a passenger train for six years after the Boston & Maine received permission to discontinue its segment of both the *Ambassador* and the *Montrealer-Washingtonian* in September 1966. Reportedly there were only nine revenue passengers on the last southbound *Washingtonian*. We can only imagine to what levels the quality of service had descended in that low ebb of fortune in New England railroading.

Today the *Montrealer* soldiers on with steady if not spectacular ridership. Given the cloudy future of Amtrak and CV, it might be best to ride it sooner rather than later.

Bibliography

Bachman, Benjamin B. "The Vermont Year." *Trains* 47,6: 36-47.

Baker, George P. *The Formation of the New England Rail Systems.* Cambridge, Mass.: Harvard University Press, 1937.

Beaudette, Edward H. *Central Vermont Railway.* Newton, N.J.: Carstens Publications, Inc., 1982.

Confalone, Mike. "Autumn Action in Northern New England." *Railfan & Railroad* 12,11: 66-70.

Hartley, Scott. "Central Vermont: A Survivor." *Trains* 51,4: 30-42.

Hastings, Philip R. *Grand Trunk Heritage.* New York: Railroad Heritage Press, 1978.

Hoagland, Wake. "How rare the Rutland." *Trains* 10,6: 12-15

Holt, Jeff. *The Grand Trunk in New England.* Toronto: Railfare Enterprises Limited, 1986.

Johnson, Ron [Editor] *Maine Central R. R. Mountain Division.* South Portland, Me.: 470 Railroad Club, undated.

Jones, Robert C. *The Central Vermont Railway* (Volumes I-VI). Silverton, Colo.: Sundance Publications Limited, 1981.

Jones, Robert C. *Railroads of Vermont* (Volumes I-II). Shelburne, Vt.: The New England Press, 1993.

Jones, Robert C., Maxfield, Whitney J., and Gove, William G. *Vermont's Granite Railroads—The Montpelier & Wells River and the Barre & Chelsea.* Boulder, Colo.: Pruett Publishing Company, 1985.

Lee, W. Storrs. *The Green Mountains of Vermont.* New York: Henry Holt and Company, 1955.

Lewis, Edward A. *Vermont's Covered Bridge Road—The Story of the St. Johnsbury & Lamoille County Railroad.* Strasburg, Pa.: The Baggage Car, 1974.

McFarlane, James R. "The Central Vermont Story—A Detailed History of the Grand Trunk's Most Extensive New England Railroad." *The Railroad Enthusiast* 10(2nd),2: 11-28.

Nelligan, Tom. *New England Shortlines.* New York: Railroad Heritage Press, 1982.

Pavlucik, Andrew J. *The New Haven Railroad—A fond look back.* New Haven: Pershing Press, 1978.

Payson, Gilbert R. Jr. "The Springfield (Vt.) Terminal Railway." *The Railroad Enthusiast* 3(1st),1: 4-5.

Shaughnessy, Jim. "White Rock and Green Hills—A Profile of Vermont's Clarendon & Pittsford Railroad." *The Railroad Enthusiast* 7(2nd),1: 3-10.

Shaughnessy, Jim. *Delaware & Hudson.* Berkeley, Calif.: Howell-North Books, 1967.

Shaughnessy, Jim. *The Rutland Road—Second Edition.* San Diego, Calif.: Howell-North Books, 1981.

Smith, Dwight A. Jr. "I Ran New England's Last Country Trolley Line." *The Railroad Enthusiast* 6(2nd),2: 3-10.

Sweetland, David R. *New England Rails 1948-1968.* Edison, N. J.: Morning Sun Books, Inc., 1989.

Some aspects of railroading never change. A brakeman on the Green Mountain Railroad is riding a cut of cars on October 8, 1993 at Bellows Falls. Mike Confalone photo.

Index

*Denotes photograph

Addison Branch 29*
Adirondacks 18*
Adnabrown Hotel 139*
Albany, N. Y. 150, 156
Alburgh, Vt. 15*, 63*
Alouette 120*, 142*, 149*, 150, 153*
Ambassador 73, 75*, 77*, 81*, 84*, 144
Amherst, Belchertown & Palmer RR 62
Amherst, Mass. 96*, 98*
Amtrak 64, 143, 146, **172**
    E-8 446 173*, 496 172*
    F-40PH 212 172*
Arlington, Vt. 49*
Atlantic & St. Lawrence RR 160, 161
Ausable, N. Y. 62

Barnet, Vt. 150
Barre & Chelsea RR 126*, 127, 128
    70-ton No. 13 126*
Barre Branch RR 126, 127
Barre RR 126, 127
Barre, Vt. 64, 73, 125, 126, 128
Bartonsville, Vt. 42*
Beecher Falls, Vt. 166, 170, 170*, 171*
Belchertown, Mass. 98*
Bellows Falls, Vt. 43*, 44*, 45*, 46*, 56*, 62, 87*, 143, 144, 144*
Bennington & Rutland RR 16, 20
Bennington, Vt. 52*, 53*
Berlin, N. H. 119, 170
Bethel, Vt. 80*
Biddeford, Me. 161
Black River 141*
Blount, Nelson 23
Bombardier, Ltd. 128
Boston & Albany RR 20, 62
Boston & Lowell RR 14, 117, 144, 148
Boston & Maine RR 23, 59, 64, 73, 118, 126, 127, 131, 138, 140, 143, **144**, 148, 161, 170
    4-6-2 Pacifics: 3696 138*, 3703 144*, 3708 32*, 3715 146*
    E-7 3800 136*
    GP-7s: 1560 145*, 1568 146*
    GP-9s: 1711 85*, 1715 146*, 1741 146*, 1743 146*, 1825 146*, 1826 85*
    Budd RDCs 145*
    Jordan Spreader 3592 145*
Boston, Mass. 73, 125, 126, 146, 148, 161, 166
Boston, Concord & Montreal RR 125, 148
Bradford, Vt. 150*
Brandon & West Rutland RR 132
Brattleboro, Vt. 62, 64, 73, 89*, 90*, 143, 144, 146
Bretton Woods, N. H. 126
Brighton, Vt. 161, 165
Brill car 60
British American Land Co. 160-161
Brooksville Bridge 13
Burlington, Vt. 21*, 22*, 24*, 25*, 60, 61, 73, 119, 125, 126

Cambridge Junction, Vt. 64, 119
Canadian National Railways 64, 161
    4-6-2 Pacific 5291 67*
    4-8-2 Mountain 6032 142*
    4-8-4 Northerns: 6173 70*, 6218 77*, 6240 65*
    C-Liners: 94*, 8706 109*, 8714 97*, 9308 66*, 9338 97*, 102*
    Dash 8-40cm 2422 165*
    H-420 78*
    Caboose 79089 112*
Canadian Northern RR 64
Canadian Pacific Railway 61, 132, 143, 146, **148**, 150, 166, 170, headquarters, St. Johnsbury 151*
    2-8-2 Mikado 5146 152*
    E-8 1800 153*, 1801 142*
    FA 4010 152*
    RS-3s: 8413 154*, 8436 154*, 8446 152*, 8453 150*
    RS-10s: 8563 154*, 8572 154*
    RS-18s: 8729 152*, 8760 154*
    RS-18m 1801 155*
    RS-18u 1866 154*
    RDC-2 9113 151*
    GP-35 5015 155*
    C-424s 4215 155*, 4241 154*, 4249 155*
Cantic, Que. 61
Castleton, Vt. 156, 157*, 158

Caverly, Gardner 20
Center Rutland, Vt. 130*, 132, 132*
Central Vermont RR 17, 20, **59**, 61, 62, 64, 117, 119, 125, 127, 143, 146, 172, reorganized as Central Vermont Railway 64
    2-8-0 Consolidations: 450 104*, 105*, 451 58*, 90*, 95*, 96*, 98*, 100*, 452 108*, 112*, 460 89*, 462 63*, 90*, 94*, 95*, 101*, 102*, 464 101*, 110*, 465 72*, 466 68*, 467 94*, 102*, 109*, 468 99*, 470 97*, 98*, 113*, 471 99*, 472 104*, 473 89*, 94*, 95*, 474 84*, 102*, 476 113*, 484 106*
    2-10-4 Texas: 703 88*, 704 68*, 84*, 85*, 707 79*, 83*, 87*, 708 87*, 88*
    4-8-2 Mountains: 602 74*, 603 68*, 72*, 83*, 92*
    GP-9s: 4445 164*, 4524 109*, 4534 109*, 4548 114*, 4549 85*, 112*, 4550 85*, 114*, 4556 96*, 4558 85*, 4923 81*, 114*, 4925 75*, 4926 114*, 4927 78*, 112*, 4929 78*
    RS-3s: 1859 77*, 1860 77*
    RS-11s: 3606 76*, 3609 76*, 3611 114*, 3612 76*
    SW-1200s: 1510 70*, 1511 70*
    Cabooses: 4011 99*, 4007 99*, 112*
    Gas-electric car No. 73, 148 66*
CERA Museum 140
Champlain & Connecticut River RR 14
Champlain & St. Lawrence RR 61
Charlestown, N. H. 131, 138, 139*, 146*
Chatham & Lebanon Valley RR 20
Chatham, N.Y. 53*, 62
Chelsea, Vt. 127
Cheshire 140, 144
Cheshire Bridge (and corporation) 138
Chester, Vt. 40*, 41*, 57*
Claremont & Concord 70-ton No. 9 137*
Claremont Junction, N. H. 87*
Clarendon & Pittsford RR 23, 131, **132**, 143, 158
    70-ton 500 133*
    GP-9 752 54*
    GP-38 203 159*
    SW-1500 502 159*
    Whitcomb center-cab No. 10 132*, 133*
Clarendon, Vt. 48*
Clement, Percival W. 158
Clyde River 153*
Colchester, Vt. 19*, 72*
Concord RR 148
Connecticut & Passumpsic Rivers RR 14, 61, 62, 117, 125, 144, 148, 150
Connecticut River 123*
Connecticut River RR 62, 126, 144
Connecticut Yankee 144
Coos Junction 166
Coos Valley RR 166
Corkscrew Division 20, 53
Cornwall Railway Light & Power Company 140
Crawford Notch, N. H. 170
CSF Acquisitions 119
Cuttingsville Trestle 40*, 57*

Danby, Vt. 55*
Danville, Vt. 122*
Danville Junction, Me. 161
Dartmouth College I and *II* 145
Day White Mountains 144, 146*
Deerfield Lumber Co. 134
Deerfield River 137*
Deerfield Valley RR 134
Delaware & Hudson RR 17, 20, 23, 62, 131, 132, 140, 143, 140, **156**, 170
    2-8-0 Double-cab "Mother Hubbard" 819 156*
    RF-16 sharks: 1205, 1216 157*
Derby, Vt. 152*
Duluth, Winnipeg & Pacific RS-11 3605 114*
Duxbury, Vt. 114*

Eagle Bridge, N. Y. 156
East Alburgh, Vt. 63*
East Barre & Chelsea RR 127
East Clarendon, Vt. 38*
East Northfield, Mass. 91*, 92*
East Ryegate, Vt. 150
East St. Johnsbury, Vt. 169*
East Swanton, Vt. 64
Emons Holding Corp. 161
Erie Canal 60
Escanaba & Lake Superior RR 157
Essex County RR 117, 118, 166
Essex Junction, Vt. 60, 64, 74*, 75*
Ethan Allen Furniture Co. 166

Fabyans, N. H. 166
Fairbanks, Erastus 117
Fisher Bridge 119, 121*

Fitchburg RR 14, 20, 134
Fitchburg, Mass. 62
Fitchville, Conn. 62, 112*
Florence, Vt. 132
Flying Yankee 140
Follett, Timothy 14
Fonda Junction, Vt. 119
Fort Edward, N. Y. 156
French Edward S. 118, 127, 140, 144

Galt, Alexander Tilloch 160
Gassetts, Vt. 56*
GATX
    GP-40 3717 164*
    SW-1500 9626 164*
Georgia High Bridge 71*
Gilbertville, Mass. 62
Gilman, Vt. 168*, 170
Ginsberg, William I. 23
Grand Trunk RR of Canada 161
Grand Trunk Pacific RR 64
Grand Trunk Railway 59, 64, 143, 148, **160**, 166
    0-6-0 No. 7530 163*, 164*
    2-8-0 Consolidation 2611 61*
    2-8-2 Mikados: 3432 2*, 3709 162*
    Diesels: 4446 82*, 4449 82*, 4905 82*, 4927 82*
Grand Trunk Western RR 75*
    4-8-2 Mountain 6039 70*, 77*
Graniteville, Vt. 124*, 128
Granville, N. Y. 157*
Great Northern Canal 14
Great Northern RR 123
Green Mountain Express 127
Green Mountain Flyer 13, 19*, 26*, 30*, 31, 32*, 38*, 40*, 43*, 48*, 73, 144, 144*
Green Mountain Railroad 23, 56-57*
    2-6-0 Mogul No. 89 57*
    RS-1s: 400 56*, 401 56*
Greenfield, Mass. 62, 135
Grout's Corner, Mass. 62
Groveton, N. H. 119, 170
Guilford Transportation Industries 64, 119, 140, 146, 170

Halifax, N. S. 161
Hardwick, Vt.121*
Harlem Extension RR 17, 62
Harriman Dam 134
Harrison, President Benjamin 126
Hays, Charles M. 64
Hercules 129*
Hereford Railway 166
Hollister Quarry 132
Holyoke, Mass. 134
Hoosac Tunnel & Wilmington RR 131, **134**
    44-ton 15 134*, 16 137*
    Double-ended snowplow 136*
Hoosac Tunnel 16, 23, 134
Hoosac Tunnel Station 134*, 135, 136*

Illinois Railroad Museum 140
Intercolonial RR 64
Interstate Commerce Act 20
Island Pond, Vt. 143, 160*, 161, 161-165*

Jay Peak 154*
Jonesville, Vt. 76*

Kennebunk, Me. 161

Lake Memphramagog 155*
Lake Winnepesauke 150
Lamoille County RR 119
Lamoille Valley RR 117, 119, 170
    RS-3m 123*
Lamoille Valley Extension RR 117
Lebanon Springs RR 17, 20
Leicester Junction, Vt. 29*
Lennoxville, Que. 148
Lewis, Edward A. 119
Lewiston, Me. 161
Lime Ridge, Que. 166
Loati, Bruno 119
Lunenburg, Vt. 118, 166
Lyndonville, Vt. 148*, 151*
Lyndonville Gas Co. 150

Magoon, Hap 150*
Maine Central RR 64, 119, 140, 143, 161, **166**
    2-6-0 367 171*
    E-7 709 169*
    GP-38s: 255 167*, 169*, 257 168*, 260 167*

City Cousins   175

GP-7 564 171*
RS-11 801 167*
U-18-B 401 169*
Maine Coast Special 161
Manchester & Lawrence RR 148
Manchester, Vt. 49*
Mansfield, Conn. 106*
Massawippi Valley RR 148
McKeesport Connecting RR 116
Mellon, Charles 126, 127
Middlebury, Vt. 28*
Miles Pond, Vt. 168*
Millers Falls, Mass. 62, 92*, 93*, 94*
Missisquoi & Clyde Rivers RR 148
Missisquoi River 70*
Missisquoi RR 62
Monongahela Railway 157
Monroe Bridge, Mass. 137*
Monson, Mass. 101-103*
Montague, Mass. 95*
Montpelier & Barre RR 128
    70-ton No. 21 124*
    S-1 No. 29 129*
    Snowplow No. 38 129*
Montpelier & St. Johnsbury RR 117
Montpelier & Wells River RR 118, 125
Montpelier, Vt. 14, 60, 64, 73, 125, 126, 127, 128, 129*
Montpelier Junction, Vt. 78*, 173*
Montreal & Plattsburgh RR 17, 62
Montreal & Vermont Junction Railway 61
Montreal, Que. 61, 62, 73, 117, 126, 146, 148, 150, 156, 160, 161, 172
Montrealer 64, 70*, 73, 78*, 143, 146, 172, 172*, 173*
Montrealer-Washingtonian 73, 144, 145, 172
Montville, Conn. 62, 111*, 112*
Morrison-Knudson Corp. 119
Morrisville, Vt. 119
Mount Royal 31
Mountain Mills, Vt. 135

Nashua & Lowell RR 148
National Transcontinental RR 64
New England Regional Commission 170
New England States Limited 73
New Hampshire & Vermont RR 119, 170
New Haven & New London RR 62
New Haven RR 20, 73, 108*, 126, 127, 144, 146
New Haven, Vt. 27*
New London, Conn. 73, 112*, 113*
New London Northern RR 16, 59, 62
New London, Willimantic & Palmer RR 62
New London, Willimantic & Springfield RR 62
New York & Canada 20
New York & Harlem RR 20
New York Central & Hudson River RR 20
New York Central RR 20, 123, 157
New York, N. Y. 62, 73, 148, 156, 172
New York, Ontario & Western RR 20
Newport & Richford RR 148, 150
Newport, Vt. 142*, 148, 149*, 150, 153*, 155*
Newsboy 97*, 101*
Newton family 134
North Amherst, Mass. 97*
North Bennington, Vt. 50*, 51*, 54*
North Derby Junction, Vt. 148
North Hero, Vt. 17*
North Stratford, Vt. 166
North Stratford RR 170
North Walpole, N. H. 47*
Northeast Kingdom 161
Northern Railroad of New Hampshire 14, 62, 148, 150
Northern Railroad of New York 14, 17, 61
Northfield, Vt. 60
Northfield, Mass. 64
Norton, Vt. 161
Norwich & Worcester RR 62
Norwich, Conn. 62

Oaks Ames 17
Ogdensburg & Lake Champlain RR 17, 62, 117
Ogdensburg Bridge & Port Authority 23
Ogdensburg grain elevator 23
Ogdensburg RR 17
Ogdensburg Transportation Co. 17
Ogdensburg, N. Y. 61, 62, 125
Olcott's Ferry 138
Old Orchard Beach, Me. 125, 161
Onion River Valley 14
Orleans, Vt. 149*
Overnighter 144

Page, John B. 16
Paine, Charles 14, 16, 59, 60, 61, 125
Palmer, Mass. 58*, 62, 64, 99-101*
Panama Canal Act 13, 20
Penn Central RR 157
Pennsylvania RR 73, 146
Pinsly, Samuel 64, 119, 128, 135
Pittsford & Rutland 132
Pittsford, Vt. 30*
Plymouth, N. H. 150
Poor, John Alfred 160
Portland & Ogdensburg RR 117, 166
Portland, Me. 117, 125, 142*, 160, 166, 170
Pownal, Vt. 146
Prince Rupert, B. C.
Proctor, Vt. 30*, 132, 133*
Providence, R. I. 64
Putney, Vt. 144

Quebec Central RR 150, 152*, 166
Quebec Junction, N. H. 166

Randolph, Vt. 79*
Readsboro, Vt. 134, 135
Red Wing 150
Rensselaer & Saratoga RR 156
Richford, Vt. 148, 150
Richford Branch 71*
Rock of Ages Corp. 116, 128,
    0-6-0s: No. 6 124*, 129*, No. 27 129*
Rockingham, Vt. 42*
Rouses Point, N. Y. 15*, 61, 64, 73
Rowe, Mass. 135
Rutland RR 13, 20, 23, 143, 158, reorganized as Rutland Railway 20
    0-6-0s: 100 36*, 106 45*, 107 22*
    2-8-0 Consolidations: 27 41*, 29 44*, 32 53*, 34 40*, 35 38*, 40*
    4-6-0 Ten Wheelers: 40 51*, 52*, 52 27*, 28*, 74 34*, 50*, 76 52*, 79 42*, 43*
    4-6-2 Pacifics: 75 43*, 80 28*, 41*, 82 37*, 38*, 83 32*, 19*, 47*, 84 18*, 85 26*, 30*
    4-8-2 Mountains: 91 40*, 92 22*, 48*, 93 33*, 34*, 44*, 47*
    RS-1s: 403 15*, 405 29*
    RS-3s: 201 25*, 36*, 204 32*, 37*, 205 22*, 42*, 208 37*
Rutland & Burlington RR 14, 16
Rutland & Canadian RR 17
Rutland & Washington RR 156
Rutland & Whitehall RR 16, 156
Rutland, Vt. 32*, 33*, 34*, 35*, 36*, 37*, 60, 61, 73, 132, 156, 158

Sacramento Northern RR 140
Saint John, N. B. 161
Salem, N. Y. 157
Salzberg, H. E. Co. 119
Saratoga, N. Y. 73
Saratoga & Washington RR 16, 156
Saratoga, N. Y. 125
Save the Rutland Club 20
Scarboro Beach, Me. 161
Shelburne, Vt. 26*
Sherbrooke, Que. 61, 148, 150
Sherman Dam 135
Shoreham, Vt. 29*
Ski Meister 73
Slack woolen goods 140
Smith, Edward C. 59
Smith, J. Gregory 59, 61, 62, 148
Smith, John 14, 59, 61
Smith, Worthington C. 61
Sortwell, Alvin F. 126
South Eastern Counties Junction Railway 148
South Royalston, Vt. 81*
Southern New England Railway 64
Springfield Electric Railway Co. 138
Springfield Terminal Railway 131, **138**
    44-ton No. 1 141*
    Steeple-cab freight motors: No. 15 140, No. 20 140, 140*
    Trolleys: No. 10 139*, No. 16 138*, 139*, No. 17 140
Springfield, Mass. 62, 73
Springfield, Vt. 130*, 131, 138, 139-141*
St. Albans, Vt. 60, 62, 67*, 68*, 69*, 70*, 73, 119
St. Armand subdivision 61, 64
St. Johns, Que. 61, 62, 64
St. Johnsbury & Lake Champlain RR 64, **117**, 127
    70-ton No. 46 120*
    Combine No. 113 116*
St. Johnsbury & Lamoille County RR 118, 119
    70-ton Nos. 46, 48 & 54 118-119*
    GP-7s: 200 121*, 122*, 201 121*, 122*

RS-3 203 123*
St. Johnsbury, Vt. 116*, 119, 122*, 148, 150, 151*, 166, 167*, 168*, 169*, 170, 171*
St. Lawrence & Atlantic 161, 164*, 165*
    GP-9 1764 165*
St. Lawrence River 160, 161
Stafford Springs, Conn. 105*
Stanstead, Sheffield & Chambly RR 61, 148
State Line, Mass. 104*
Steamtown 23
Sterzing, Bruce 157
Sullivan County RR 62, 144
Sunday River Silver Bullet Ski Express 165*
Sutton, Vt. 154*
Swanton, Vt. 65*, 117, 119

Titanic 64
Travelers Express car 61 134*
Troy & Boston RR 16
Twin State RR 119, 170

U. S. Filter Corp. 170
U. S. Supreme Court 64, 143, 146
United States Railway Administration 20
Upper Coos RR 166

Van Dyke, George 166
Vanderbuilt, William H. 20
Vergennes, Vt. 27*
Vermont & Canada RR 14, 16, 59, 60, 61
Vermont & Massachusetts RR 14, 16, 17, 62
Vermont Central RR 14, 16, 17, 59, 61, 62, 73, 148
Vermont Historical Society 23
Vermont Marble Co. 131, 132
Vermont Northern RR 119
Vermont Public Service Commission 23
Vermont Railway 23, 54-55*, 133, 143, 158
    GP-38-2s: 201 55*, 202 54*, 159*
    RS-1 404 55*
Vermont Transportation Authority 119, 128
Vermont Valley RR 16, 17, 62, 126, 127, 144
Vermonter 79*
Vernon, Vt. 115*

Wallingford, Vt. 49*
Waloomsac, N. Y. 54*
Ware River RR 62
Washington County RR Corp. 128
Washingtonian 172
Waterbury, Vt. 77*
Waterloo & Magog RR 61
Waterloo, Que.
Webb, Dr. William Seward 20
Wells River, Vt. 125, 126*, 127, 128, 144, 146, 150, 153*
West Alburgh, Vt. 60
West Braintree, Vt. 78*
West Farnham, Que. 148
West Hartford, Vt. 83*
West River RR 64
West Rutland, Vt. Saint John, N. B. 132, 133*
Western RR 62
Western Vermont RR 16
Westminster, Vt. 88*
Whippet, The 20
White Mountain Express 31, 73, 125
White Mountains 73
White River Junction, Vt. 64, 73, 83-85*, 144, 145*, 146, 147*, 150, 151*, 172
White River Valley 14
Whitefield, N. H. 119, 170
Whitehall & Plattsburgh 17, 62
Whitehall, N. Y. 133, 156
Williamstown, Mass. 64
Willimantic, Conn. 108*, 109*, 110*
Wilmington, Vt. 134
Windsor, Vt. 62, 64, 125, 144, 146
Winooski, Vt. 61, 76*
Wolcott, Vt. 120*
Woodsville, N. H. 170

Yarmouth Junction, Me. 161

...My Dad took me down to the old Salem depot where we caught a steam t
on the right side of the car and watching the locomotive headlight illuminate t
as we rushed past them. I remember, too, the glorious luminosity of the greer
face, the intoxicating sulfury smell from the locomotive, and the crystal stars